Quiet Places:
The Burial Sites of Civil War Generals in Tennessee

BY
BUCKNER AND NATHANIEL C. HUGHES, JR.

EAST TENNESSEE HISTORICAL SOCIETY

ISBN 0-941199-10-X

PREFACE

W E PREPARED THIS BOOK FOR THOSE WHO WOULD VISIT OUR STATE and search for the military leaders of the more than 180,000 Tennesseans who fought for the Union and the Confederacy. Sixty-three individuals are included. These general officers of such diverse backgrounds happen to have been buried in Tennessee. They were determined, for various reasons, to protect and promote the causes in which they believed. For equally different reasons they rose to the rank of general. Some had absolutely no business holding positions of command, while others displayed astonishing aptitude. Fourteen of them (thirteen Confederates) perished during the war—nine were killed by the enemy, one by a fellow officer. Three would die later of natural causes, another mysteriously.

We were liberal in our definition of general officer. Eighteen of these men will not be found in Ezra Warner's classic *Generals in Blue* and *Generals in Gray*. But we felt justified including them, since they were either brevet generals or for other reasons presented in their individual sketches. We realize our bite-size biographies will leave some readers hungering for more information. We hope so.

About half of the generals included in this work are buried in the major cemeteries of Memphis and Nashville. Others are in plots scattered about the state. To visit their graves leads one into towns and sections of Tennessee off the beaten path. The familiar is reordered, refreshed. We always looked forward to these outings of discovery. Sometimes, however, the search saddened us. We would shake our heads over the deaths of promising young men and feel the bitter disappointment, yet great pride, of those who risked so much. Nevertheless, we had an enjoyable time locating the graves of the generals and learning about them as individuals. Each man seemed unique to us; certainly, each had a different story.

The quest led us into delightful spots and introduced us to many kind, entertaining, and helpful people. We ended our work loving Tennessee even more. It is such a beautiful land. It is our hope, our purpose, in preparing this book, that others may visit these *quiet places* and thereby come to a fuller appreciation of our state and our forebears.

Summer 1992

Bucky and Nat Hughes, Jr.
Chattanooga

ACKNOWLEDGEMENTS

WE GRATEFULLY APPRECIATE THE ENTHUSIASM AND EFFORT OF W. Todd Groce, Executive Director of the East Tennessee Historical Society, and R. B. Rosenburg, Managing Editor of *The Journal of East Tennessee History*, without whose assistance this book would have remained only an interesting idea that Jack Dunlap of Harahan, La., suggested.

The photographs of the generals appearing in this volume have been derived from the following sources and repositories: Francis T. Miller, ed., *The Photographic History of the Civil War* (10 vols., N.Y., 1911); Clement A. Evans, ed., *Confederate Military History* (12 vols., Atlanta, 1899); Tennessee State Library and Archives; Special Collections Library, The University of Tennessee, Knoxville; *Confederate Veteran* magazine; J. Harvey Mathes, *The Old Guard in Gray* (Memphis, 1897); William R. Carter, *History of the First Regiment of Tennessee Volunteer Cavalry* (Knoxville, 1902); Chattanooga-Hamilton County Bicentennial Library; and John B. Lindsley, *The Military Annals of Tennessee* (Nashville, 1886). The photographs of the burial sites are our own creations.

So many people have helped us—policemen, groundskeepers, funeral home directors, secretaries in county court houses, and other Tennesseans along the road who gladly gave us directions. Certain individuals who provided specific information must be mentioned here: Marylin Bell Hughes, Tennessee State Library and Archives, Nashville; The Rev. Ernest D. Cushman, Chattanooga; J. Spencer Culberson, Franklin, Tenn.; Ron L. Hale, Forrest Hills Cemetery, Chattanooga; Ms. Elizabeth Robnett, Pikeville, Tenn.; Roy Morris, Jr., Chattanooga; A. F. Tate, Jr., Pulaski, Tenn.; Jim Wallace, Chattanooga National Cemetery; Robin Schenk, Mt. Olivet Cemetery, Nashville; T. C. Peulausk, Chattanooga-Chickamauga National Military Park; Mary Ann Monk, National Park Service, Greeneville, Tenn.; Neil Coulter, Lupton Library, University of Tennessee, Chattanooga; Charles Arp, Ohio Historical Society, Columbus; Jim Tingen, Chattanooga-Hamilton County Bicentennial Library; Patricia M. LaPointe, Memphis/Shelby County Public Library; Martha K. Griffin, Elmwood Cemetery, Memphis; Janet Smotherman, Bridgeview Black and White Photo Lab; E. Cheryl Schnirring, Illinois State Historical Library; Alix Dempster, Old Gray Cemetery, Knoxville; and David Babelay, Knoxville.

B. & N. H., Jr.

Quiet Places

★ CHARLES WILLIAM ADAMS ★
Brigadier General, CSA

*B*orn August 16, 1817, in Newburyport, Mass., of distinguished stock, Adams migrated in 1819 with his parents to New Albany, Ind. There he received his basic education and was apprenticed to a store owner for five years. When he was eighteen, Adams moved to Helena, Ark., where he worked in a store and later became a bank cashier. He read law and was admitted to the bar in Helena in 1839. In 1852 he was elected judge of the First Judicial District of Arkansas and served two years. An old-line Whig, Adams took an active role in the secession convention in March 1861.

Adams' Civil War career began as quartermaster on the staff of Thomas H. Bradley (*q.v.*). Then, in the fall of 1861, Adams raised his own regiment, the 23rd Arkansas Infantry, which he led at Island No. 10 and Corinth. Failing to be retained as regimental commander when the Army of Tennessee reorganized, Adams became chief of staff for Gen. Thomas C. Hindman. In this capacity he performed with "conspicuous gallantry" at Missionary Ridge and, as a result, was promoted to brigadier general. He served the remainder of the war in the northern subdivision of the Trans-Mississippi theater.

Following the war Adams returned to Helena, but he was prohibited by the military authorities from practicing law. He moved to Memphis in the fall of 1865 and became a law partner of his close friend, Albert Pike. He practiced in Memphis until his death of yellow fever on September 10, 1878.

Adams' only daughter, Kate, married a former Confederate officer, Capt. Arthur H. Keller. Their daughter was Helen Keller.

BURIAL SITE: On the same lot with his law partner, Judge L. V. Dixon, South Grove Section, Elmwood Cemetery, Memphis. Exit Interstate 240 (Exit #29) onto Crump (Lamar) Blvd. Proceed 2 blocks (.2 mi.) west to Dudley. Turn left (south) and continue down Dudley .5 mi. over the elevated bridge entrance to the cemetery.

★ JOHN ADAMS ★
Brigadier General, CSA

*B*orn in Nashville, July 1, 1825, Adams was raised in Pulaski, Tenn. He attended West Point, graduating in 1846 and receiving a commission in the First Dragoons. With this regiment in Mexico, he won brevet promotion and distinction at Santa Cruz de Rosales. He continued in the regular army until the outbreak of the Civil War, serving in frontier posts in California and the southwest. Adams later became a recruiting officer and for a while aide to the governor of Minnesota.

In 1861 he entered the Confederate army, receiving a commission as captain of cavalry. He served in Memphis, western Kentucky, and Mississippi, being promoted to colonel in May 1862 and given a brigade of cavalry, with which he saw action in North Alabama and Middle Tennessee. He became a brigadier general on December 29 of that same year. After the death of Lloyd Tilghman, Adams assumed command of his Mississippi infantry brigade and led it under Joseph E. Johnston and Leonidas Polk in Mississippi throughout most of 1863. He capably commanded the brigade as a part of Polk's corps in the Atlanta campaign, remaining with the Army of Tennessee in Hood's ill-fated invasion of Tennessee. At Franklin he was wounded early in the fight, but refused to leave the field. Leading his men in their desperate charge, he fell mortally wounded as he attempted to leap his horse over the enemy breastworks. Adams died on the field in the hands of his captors.

BURIAL SITE: Old Maplewood Cemetery, Pulaski. From intersection of U.S. Highways 31 and 64, go 1/4 mi. east on East College Street (U.S. 64). Turn right (south) on Sam Davis Avenue. Cemetery is on right (west side), approximately 300 yds. Adams' grave is without an upright marker, in Adams-Nelson plot (marked with large cross) in north central section, some 30 yds. east of monument to Gen. John C. Brown (*q.v.*).

★ JAMES PATTON ANDERSON ★
Major General, CSA

A native Tennessean, though usually identified with Florida, Anderson was born near Winchester in Franklin County, February 16, 1822. He graduated from Jefferson College in Pennsylvania, then moved to Kentucky where he studied law. He was admitted to the bar and practiced for a short while in Hernando, Miss. When the Mexican War came, at the age of twenty-five, he commanded a battalion of the Mississippi Rifles. He returned to the Magnolia State and served one term in the legislature, before venturing in 1853 to the far west as U.S. marshal in the Washington Territory. Anderson later represented that area in Congress (1855-57). President James Buchanan appointed him governor of the territory in 1857, but he declined the position, choosing instead to manage his plantation near Monticello, Fla. He served in the Florida secession convention, and at the outbreak of the war became colonel of the 1st Florida Infantry. Initially, he served under Braxton Bragg at Pensacola and became brigadier general, February 10, 1862.

Anderson effectively commanded a brigade at Shiloh and a division at Perryville. He won commendation at Murfreesboro and again led a division at Chickamauga and Chattanooga. He became a major general on February 17, 1864, and was placed in command of the District of Florida. He returned to the Army of Tennessee in late summer 1864, leading a division at Ezra Church and Jonesboro. Because of a wound received at Jonesboro, he missed John B. Hood's Tennessee campaign, but was again in action at Bentonville the following spring.

After the war Anderson located in Memphis, where he collected taxes for Shelby County and edited an agricultural publication. He died in Memphis, September 20, 1872.

BURIAL SITE: Fowler Section, Elmwood Cemetery, Memphis. Exit Interstate 240 (Exit #29) onto Crump (Lamar) Blvd. Proceed 2 blocks (.2 mi.) west to Dudley. Turn left (south) and continue down Dudley .5 mi. over the elevated bridge entrance to the cemetery.

★ SAMUEL READ ANDERSON ★
Brigadier General, CSA

Son of a Revolutionary War officer, Anderson was born in Bedford County, Va., on February 17, 1804. His restless family came to Kentucky when he was quite young. He lived in Giles and Sumner counties and ultimately settled in Davidson. When the Mexican War came, Anderson helped organize the First Tennessee regiment and became its lieutenant colonel. Anderson involved himself deeply in political life and, as a prominent Middle Tennessee Democrat, became known by a less than admiring Andrew Johnson as one of the Nashville "Post Office Clique." He did serve as postmaster of Nashville (1853-61) and as cashier of the Bank of Tennessee for a number of years.

When Tennessee created its Provisional Army in May 1861, Anderson was named by Democratic Gov. Isham G. Harris as one of its two major generals. In July 1861 Anderson became a brigadier general in the Confederate army, and he was assigned to command a brigade comprised of the 1st, 7th, and 14th Tennessee infantry regiments. As brigade commander he participated in Robert E. Lee's West Virginia campaign of 1861 and served under Thomas J. "Stonewall" Jackson in the Romney campaign. For a time he commanded the Tennessee brigade under Magruder in the Peninsula campaign, but ill health forced him from the field and into retirement in the late spring of 1862. Anderson returned from retirement in late 1864, taking charge of operations of the bureau of conscription in Tennessee, though his office was in Selma, Ala.

Following the war Anderson returned to Nashville, where he worked in the mercantile business until his death on January 2, 1883.

BURIAL SITE: Old City Cemetery, Nashville. Interstates 40/65 to Exit 210C. One block south to intersection of Nolensville Pike (4th Avenue South) and Oak Street. Within the cemetery the grave is at the intersection of Oak and City Avenues.

★ WILLIAM BRIMAGE BATE ★
Major General, CSA

*B*orn at a pioneer settlement near Bledsoe's Lick (now Castalian Springs) on October 7, 1826, Bate left home at age sixteen and took the road to adventure. He worked on a steamboat up and down the Cumberland and Mississippi Rivers until the Mexican War began, when he volunteered to serve in a Louisiana regiment. In 1847 he became a first lieutenant in the 3rd Tennessee Infantry. When he returned to Tennessee after the war, Bate established a Democratic newspaper in Gallatin and in 1849 was elected at age twenty-three to the Tennessee Assembly. He then turned to the study of law and opened his practice in Gallatin. In 1854 he became attorney general of the Nashville district and served until 1860. In that year he became an elector for the Breckinridge ticket.

Bate was active in the secession movement and quickly became colonel of the 2nd Tennessee Infantry. He fought at Shiloh, where he was badly wounded but won commendations from Patrick Cleburne and William J. Hardee. On October 3, 1862, came promotion to brigadier general, and he returned to the field in time for the Tullahoma campaign during the summer of 1863. At Chickamauga his brigade in Stewart's division performed conspicuously well, as they did two months later at Missionary Ridge. Bate was promoted to major general, February 23, 1864, and led a division capably in the Atlanta campaign in Hardee's corps. He continued his steady, dependable service throughout Hood's invasion of Tennessee and was with the Army of Tennessee in its last fight at Bentonville.

Following the war he resumed the practice of law in Nashville and became prominent in state politics, serving as a member of the Tennessee Democratic executive committee, as delegate to the national Democratic convention, and as a Tilden-Hendricks elector. In 1882 Bate was elected governor and again two years later. In 1886 he was elected senator and served in that capacity until his death in Washington, D.C., on March 9, 1905.

BURIAL SITE: Section 6, Mount Olivet Cemetery, Nashville. Take Lebanon Pike (U.S. 70) east beyond Fessler's Lane. Cemetery is easily identifiable on right (south).

★ WILLIAM NELSON RECTOR BEALL ★
Brigadier General, CSA

A native of Bardstown, Ky., Beall was born on March 20, 1825. As a youth he moved with his parents to Arkansas and from there entered West Point. Upon graduation in 1848, he was assigned to the 4th U.S. Infantry and served with his regiment on the northwest frontier until 1850. He next became an officer with the 5th Infantry, seeing extensive duty in Texas and the Indian Territory until 1861.

After resigning his commission in March 1861 and becoming a captain in the regular Confederate forces, he served in Arkansas under Earl Van Dorn. The following March came promotion to colonel and a month later brigadier general, with command of all cavalry of the army at Corinth. He took temporary command of Port Hudson in September 1862 and fought at that post, in charge of an Arkansas-Mississippi brigade, until Port Hudson's surrender the following July. Imprisoned at Johnson's Island, he became in 1864 an agent of the Confederate government in charge of Confederate prisoners of war, with an office in New York City. He sold cotton, which was permitted to pass through the Federal blockade, to secure necessary medicine, clothing, and especially blankets, for his unfortunate comrades. Beall, himself, was finally exchanged in August 1865.

After the war he located in St. Louis and became a merchant. Beall died in McMinnville, Tenn., on July 25, 1883.

BURIAL SITE: Section 1, Mount Olivet Cemetery, Nashville. Take Lebanon Pike (U.S. 70) east beyond Fessler's Lane. Cemetery is easily identifiable on right (south) side.

Photo not available

★ THOMAS H. BRADLEY ★
Major General, Arkansas State Troops

*B*orn July 25, 1808, in Williamson County, Tenn., Bradley became a merchant in Franklin, then migrated in 1842 to Crittenden County, Ark., and established a plantation just upriver from Memphis. Bradley fought in the Seminole War with the rank of major of volunteers, but returned to planting in Eastern Arkansas, accumulating great wealth, many slaves, and much land. He loved horses and was president of the Memphis Jockey Club in 1858. A secessionist leader, he participated actively in the Arkansas secession convention in March 1861.

Arkansas turned to Bradley in the late spring of 1861 and made him a major general of state forces. As such he operated in eastern Arkansas in the summer of 1861, but his attempt at military leadership was a disaster, his troops fleeing at the false report of an enemy approach. Bradley's officers, including Patrick Cleburne, tried every expedient to escape serving under his command. Finally, in the fall of 1861, citing age and physical infirmities, Bradley disappeared from the military scene. He died during the war, on September 30, 1864, probably at his home in Crittenden County.

BURIAL SITE: Chapel Hill Section, Elmwood Cemetery, Memphis. Exit Interstate 240 (Exit #29) onto Crump (Lamar) Blvd. Proceed 2 blocks (.2 mi.) west to Dudley. Turn left (south) and continue down Dudley .5 mi. over the elevated bridge entrance to the cemetery.

★ JOHN CALVIN BROWN ★
Major General, CSA

*B*orn January 6, 1827, in Giles County, Brown graduated from Jackson College in Columbia and read law for two years, practicing in Pulaski until 1861. A Whig, he served as presidential elector for the moderate Bell-Everett ticket in 1860. He became in May 1861 colonel of the 3rd Tennessee Infantry and commanded a brigade at Fort Donelson, where he was captured. On August 30, 1862, shortly after his exchange, he was promoted to brigadier general. He participated in Bragg's Kentucky campaign, being wounded at Perryville, and was again wounded at Chickamauga, though he recovered in time to take part in the fight at Missionary Ridge. Brown played a conspicuous role in the Atlanta campaign, being promoted to major general on August 4, 1864. He commanded a division under Frank Cheatham (*q.v.*) at Franklin, where he was severely wounded, but managed to rejoin the Army of Tennessee before its surrender.

After the war Brown returned to the practice of law in Pulaski. In 1870 he became the grand master of Tennessee Masons and also presided over the state constitutional convention. He became governor in 1870, the first Democrat elected governor of Tennessee after the war, and was re-elected in 1872. He is noted for having sharply reduced the indebtedness of the state and restoring its credit. Defeated for the Senate in 1875 by Andrew Johnson (*q.v.*), he became active in railroad expansion and president of two railroads. He died in Red Boiling Springs, Tenn., August 17, 1889.

BURIAL SITE: Old Maplewood Cemetery, Pulaski. From intersection of U.S. Highways 31 and 64 go 1/4 mile east on East College Street (U.S. 64). Turn right (south) on Sam Davis Avenue. Cemetery is on right (west side), approximately 300 yds., in northcentral section.

★ JAMES PATTON BROWNLOW ★
Brevet Brigadier General, USA

Son of Tennessee's most controversial governor, William G. ("Parson") Brownlow, James P. Brownlow was born December 17, 1842, in upper East Tennessee, at Jonesboro. He attended Emory and Henry College in southwest Virginia, then read law with John Bell. When war came Brownlow rode through Confederate lines to Cumberland Gap, where he joined the Union army as a private and helped organize a company of East Tennesseans. He became captain in the 4th Tennessee Infantry, USA, and continued as such while the regiment was stationed near Cumberland Gap. When the 4th became the 1st Tennessee Cavalry at Camp Denison, Ohio, November 1, 1862, Brownlow was elected as lieutenant colonel.

After Col. Robert Johnson (*q.v.*) soon absented himself from the regiment, Brownlow took charge, leading it in the Tullahoma campaign in the summer of 1863 as part of Rosecrans' 1st Cavalry Division under Edward McCook. Brownlow and his regiment performed creditably in North Alabama, and at Chickamauga did good work protecting wagon trains. In October 1863, during Gen. Joseph Wheeler's raid into Middle Tennessee, Brownlow pursued Wheeler's Confederate troopers so closely as to capture "Little Joe's" cap.

The 1st Tennessee moved to Kingston in late November 1863 and had sharp engagements in pursuit of Gen. James Longstreet's forces at Hay's Ferry and Mossy Creek, both times outnumbered and once surrounded. Brownlow displayed outstanding leadership extricating his men from these dangerous fights. Following more action in East Tennessee, Brownlow and his men participated actively throughout the Atlanta campaign, and in the late phases Brownlow acted as brigade commander, winning a commission as brevet brigadier.

The regiment once more returned to Middle Tennessee, and in a cavalry fight against troopers under N. B. Forrest (*q.v.*) near Franklin, Brownlow was shot through both thighs. The tall 6' 6" Brownlow was attended by Dr. Daniel B. Cliffe of Franklin, a former Confederate surgeon but turned-Union sympathizer. In due course Brownlow fell in love and married Cliffe's daughter, Belle.

Outspoken himself, young Brownlow always stood by his doting father, who criticized President Andrew Johnson in 1866, when the government recognized James by sending him on a special mission to San Francisco. In 1867, in the days when the Ku Klux Klan threatened Union men throughout the state, Brownlow's father appointed his son as adjutant general of Tennessee. Afterwards, James tried a number of civilian jobs: printer, railroad superintendent, and farmer. Following his wife's death in 1878, he returned to East Tennessee and died on April 26, 1879, in Knoxville, at the age of 37.

BURIAL SITE: Rest Haven Cemetery, Franklin. From square go north out 4th Ave. approximately .2 mi. Rest Haven is on left at intersection of 4th Ave. and N. Margin St. Enter at main gate on 4th, go to 5th aisle of graves, 3rd plot to left (south). Cliffe plot is enclosed by iron fence.

★ ALEXANDER WILLIAM CAMPBELL ★
Brigadier General, CSA

*B*orn in Nashville, June 4, 1828, Campbell attended West Tennessee College, studied law at Cumberland University in Lebanon, and opened his practice in Jackson, Tenn. When war broke out he served as a staff officer under Frank Cheatham (*q.v.*), until becoming in October 1861 colonel of the 33rd Tennessee Infantry. This West Tennessee regiment remained inactive in Union City until January 1862, when it marched to Columbus, Ky. At Shiloh the 33rd fought well and won the praise of Leonidas Polk. Campbell was wounded severely and, despite his service, was not re-elected colonel in May 1862, when the 33rd was reorganized. He remained with the army, however, as a supernumerary, and took charge of the ordnance train as the Army of Tennessee slowly retreated from Kentucky.

Just before the battle of Murfreesboro, Campbell was appointed adjutant and inspector general for Polk's corps and remained in this capacity until spring 1863, when he became a principal subordinate of Gideon Pillow (*q.v.*) in the Volunteer and Conscript Bureau. In this capacity he was captured in West Tennessee in July 1863 and confined at Johnson's Island. When exchanged the following year, he was promoted to brigadier general, served Nathan Bedford Forrest (*q.v.*) as inspector general, assumed command of a cavalry brigade in West Tennessee under William Hicks Jackson (*q.v.*), and remained in command until the end of the war.

Campbell returned to Jackson after the war and resumed his law practice. He became active in the Knights Templar and the Knights of Pythias, and in 1880 decided to run as a Democrat for governor, but was unsuccessful. He died in Jackson, June 13, 1893.

BURIAL SITE: Riverside Cemetery, Jackson. Leave Interstate 40 at Exit #82A and take U.S. 45 (North Highland) into the square in Jackson. Turn right on Chester Street and proceed two blocks to Riverside. Turn left and go one block. Campbell's grave is in south central portion.

★ WILLIAM BOWEN CAMPBELL ★
Brigadier General, USA

*B*orn February 1, 1807, on Mansker's Creek, near Hendersonville, Sumner County, Tenn., Campbell read law in Virginia under his uncle David Campbell and Henry St. George Tucker, and opened his practice in Carthage, Tenn. He represented Smith County in the General Assembly (1835-36), before ably leading a company of Tennesseans in the Seminole War. Upon his return Campbell ran for Congress as a Whig, defeating the popular candidate William Trousdale. Following three consecutive terms in Washington, Campbell gave up his seat to become colonel of the First Tennessee in the Mexican War. He and his regiment served most effectively in northern Mexico and in the fighting from Vera Cruz to Cerro Gordo.

After returning from Mexico, he was elected governor of Tennessee, serving one term, but he declined to run again. In 1853 he moved to Lebanon, Tenn., where he became president of the Bank of Middle Tennessee and farmed. Like most Tennessee Whigs, Campbell opposed secession in 1861 and campaigned against it. When war broke out, he was offered commissions in both armies. He accepted Abraham Lincoln's offer and became brigadier general in the Union army in June 1862, "with the understanding there would be no active duty."

He once again was elected to Congress as a conservative Unionist in August 1865 but was denied his seat until July 1866, when Tennessee was readmitted to the Union. He died near Lebanon on August 19, 1867.

BURIAL SITE: Cedar Grove Cemetery, Lebanon. Follow U.S. 231 into town square of Lebanon, go west on Main Street (Business U.S. 70) one block, turn left (south) on South Maple Street and proceed 1 mi. Old cemetery is on left. Enter Gate #1 (last gate away from city). Grave within fifty feet of South Maple St. on right (southwestern corner of cemetery).

★ WILLIAM HENRY CARROLL ★
Brigadier General, CSA

*B*orn in Nashville about 1810, Carroll was the son of one of Tennessee's most popular governors, William Carroll. Young William tried the life of a plantation owner in Panola County, Miss., before relocating to Memphis in 1848. For a while he was a banker and broker, then became postmaster and served in that capacity until the outbreak of the war. He was an important member of the Democratic party in Tennessee, participating in several national conventions, the Nashville Convention (1850), and the Tennessee constitutional convention (1861).

Commissioned brigadier general in the Provisional Army of Tennessee, he was accepted into the Confederate army as colonel, 37th Tennessee Infantry, rising in rank to brigadier general in October 1861. After Albert Sidney Johnston ordered him to troubled East Tennessee in the late fall, Carroll took charge of the section, proclaimed martial law, and attempted vigorously to suppress opposition to the Confederacy. Carroll and his brigade fought at Mill Springs in January 1862, and he was commended by George B. Crittenden for his efforts. Braxton Bragg took a different view, however, and soon ordered Carroll arrested for "drunkenness, incompetency, and neglect." Dispirited, Carroll resigned his commission the following February and joined his family which had fled to Canada. There he remained after the war and died, in Montreal, on May 3, 1868.

BURIAL SITE: Lenow Circle Section, Elmwood Cemetery, Memphis. Exit Interstate 240 (Exit #29) onto Crump (Lamar) Blvd. Proceed 2 blocks (.2 mi.) west to Dudley. Turn left (south) and continue down Dudley .5 mi. over the elevated bridge entrance to the cemetery.

★ JOHN CARPENTER CARTER ★
Brigadier General, CSA

*B*orn at Waynesboro, Ga., December 19, 1837, Carter attended the University of Virginia, then read law under his father-in-law-to-be, Judge Abram Caruthers, at Cumberland University in Lebanon. Carter taught law at Cumberland, then moved to Memphis, where he practiced until the outbreak of the war. He became captain, 38th Tennessee Infantry, and performed notably at Shiloh, Murfreesboro, and Chickamauga, winning rapid promotion. At Perryville he led his regiment and won commendation from his division commander, Benjamin F. Cheatham (*q.v.*). At Murfreesboro, Carter's 38th, though outmanned, fought spectacularly, capturing more than five hundred prisoners.

During the Atlanta campaign Carter commanded the Tennessee brigade of Marcus J. Wright, and he was promoted to brigadier general on July 7, 1864. He commanded Cheatham's division at Jonesboro. As brigade commander during Hood's Tennessee campaign under John C. Brown (*q.v.*), he assaulted the enemy works at Franklin and was mortally wounded, dying two weeks later on December 10, 1864, at the Harrison home, several miles south of Franklin.

BURIAL SITE: Rose Hill, Columbia. From court house on square in Columbia, go south 1/4 mi. on U.S. 31 to Main Street. Turn left and proceed east a short distance. Main St. becomes Cemetery St., which leads directly to Rose Hill.

Photo not available

★ WILLIAM RICHARD CASWELL ★
Brigadier General, Provisional Army of Tennessee

*B*orn in Tennessee in 1809 of a distinguished North Carolina family, Caswell graduated in 1828 from the University of Nashville. He read law and began his practice in Jefferson County. Popular and politically active, he became involved in the militia, attaining in 1835 the rank of colonel. In 1842 he became an assignee in bankruptcy for thirteen East Tennessee counties and the following year attorney general for the Twelfth Judicial Circuit. The Mexican War interrupted his life and he immediately organized a company of Knox County cavalry. As they journeyed west, Caswell came upon his University of Nashville classmate, Gideon Pillow (*q.v.*), who offered him a position on his staff. Caswell soon tired of staff duty, however, and sought a more active military role with his old company in the 1st Tennessee Mounted Volunteers. Following the war he resumed his work as attorney general, serving until 1855, when he became assistant cashier of the Dandridge, Tenn., bank. He also was a director of the East Tennessee and Virginia Railroad and a large landholder, owning property in Iowa as well as Tennessee. As a slaveholder he was outspoken in his views about East Tennessee supporting the Confederacy.

When the Provisional Army of Tennessee was organized in early 1861, Caswell was named as one of five brigadier generals, commanding troops in East Tennessee. The Confederate War Department, however, did not offer him a commission when the Tennessee army was absorbed. Caswell had made many bitter enemies with his views and by his participation in the trial of East

Tennessee bridge-burners. On August 6, 1862, he was brutally murdered by a gang of men near his home.

BURIAL SITE: Facing main circle, Old Gray Cemetery, Knoxville. Exit Interstate 40 on Highway 441 at Convention Center Exit. Proceed east into Knoxville until traffic light at Broadway. Turn left and proceed .5 mi. Cemetery on left opposite St. John's Lutheran Church.

★ JAMES RONALD CHALMERS ★
Brigadier General, CSA

A native of Halifax County Va., Chalmers was born January 11, 1831. Reared in Holly Springs, Miss., he was graduated from South Carolina College in Columbia before returning to Holly Springs, where he practiced law and was elected district attorney in 1858. Three years later he was chosen a delegate of the Mississippi secession convention.

Chalmers rose rapidly in rank during the Civil War, becoming a brigadier general on February 13, 1862. He served first in Florida before coming north with Braxton Bragg's forces in time for Shiloh. In that battle Chalmers won high praise from his division commander, Jones M. Withers, and from Bragg himself. For a while he commanded a cavalry brigade with the Army of Tennessee, until illness forced him back to his infantry unit. He lost Bragg's favor in September 1862, however, with an injudicious attack on a Federal blockhouse. Then, at Murfreesboro, his brigade suffered high casualties and Chalmers himself fell wounded. In 1863 he was again transferred to the cavalry, operating for the remainder of the war in North Mississippi and in West Tennessee. His service under N. B. Forrest (*q.v.*) as a brigade and division commander was effective, sometimes conspicuously so, though the relationship between the two generals was often stormy.

Following the war Chalmers resumed the practice of law at Friar's Point, Miss., and later in Sardis. In 1876 he became a state senator and later that year was elected to Congress. Over the next twelve years he served in the House, although his elections were usually disputed and he was twice denied his seat. In 1888 Chalmers moved to Memphis, where he practiced law until his death on April 9, 1898.

BURIAL SITE: Evergreen Section, Elmwood Cemetery, Memphis. Exit Interstate 240 (Exit #29) onto Crump (Lamar) Blvd. Proceed 2 blocks (.2 mi.) west to Dudley. Turn left (south) and continue down Dudley .5 mi. over the elevated bridge entrance to the cemetery.

★ THOMAS EMMET CHAMPION ★
Brevet Brigadier General, USA

*B*orn in Palmyra, Wayne County, N.Y., on August 3, 1825, Champion attended common schools, before emigrating at the age of twelve with his family to Michigan. There he worked with his father on a farm until he was sixteen years of age. He next helped in a printing shop, spending his spare time studying medicine. Entering the University of Michigan, he earned his medical degree and began practicing in 1847. After his marriage the following year, Champion moved first to Freeport, Ill., in 1850, and the next year to Warren, Ill. Although a practicing physician, he studied law and was admitted to the Illinois bar in 1856. Ultimately, he abandoned medicine, though many considered him a successful physician.

When war came Champion raised a company, which became part of the 96th Illinois, and he was elected colonel of that regiment, owing to his "commanding presence" and "admirable voice." Ironically, his men "suffered severely" from camp diseases while on duty in Kentucky and Tennessee in 1862-63. At one point, when the surgeon and second assistant surgeon became ill, Champion detailed a physician company commander to assist the first assistant surgeon, while he devoted himself to protecting his troops from lawsuits arising from foraging.

Champion distinguished himself as a combat officer. At Chickamauga, he beat back attacks on Snodgrass Hill, while sustaining heavy losses; and later, at Lookout Mountain, he led his troops in a successful assault. Champion moved up to brigade command during the Atlanta campaign, but in June 1864, at Kennesaw Mountain, he received a severe facial wound. Poor health, which had interrupted and limited his service after December 1862, took its toll in the fall of 1864. Champion left active field duty and became a member of a military commission in Nashville, whose purpose was to try "officers and soldiers charged with breaches of military regulations." Appointed a brevet brigadier in February 1865, he resigned from the army the following June.

In 1865, Champion and his family settled in Knoxville, Tenn., where he opened a law practice with Col. John Baxter. Five years later he formed another partnership with M. L. Hall. Respected for his legal scholarship and judgment, he suffered from tuberculosis, which limited his activity and eventually led to his death in Knoxville, on June 13, 1873.

BURIAL SITE: Old Gray Cemetery, Knoxville. Exit I-40 on US #441 at Convention Center Exit. Proceed east into Knoxville until stoplight at Broadway. Turn left and proceed .5 mi. Cemetery on left opposite St. John's Lutheran Church. Turn right immediately after entering cemetery. Wind down hill, turn right, then take left fork. Proceed about 50 yds. Grave on left (west) side of road, third tier of graves from road.

★ BENJAMIN FRANKLIN CHEATHAM ★
Lieutenant General, CSA

Cheatham was born in Nashville, on October 20, 1820, to a family of prominent and influential Democrats. Early a member of the militia, he was captain of the popular Nashville Blues, and with this company he went to Mexico in 1846. He served with distinction and returned home to raise a regiment himself, then raced back to Mexico in time for Winfield Scott's final push against Mexico City. After several years in California, Cheatham returned to Tennessee and won recognition as an innovative farmer.

At the outbreak of the war, Cheatham helped organize the Provisional Army of Tennessee and became a brigadier, first in that army, then on July 9, 1861, in the Confederate army. Cheatham operated in southeast Missouri in the late summer, captured Hickman, Ky., in September, and at Belmont, on November 7, he distinguished himself in a counterattack that saved the day. He became on March 10, 1862, major general and with his division of Tennesseans he served under Leonidas Polk at Shiloh, Perryville, Murfreesboro, and Chickamauga. He was Polk's most trusted lieutenant.

At Missionary Ridge and throughout the Atlanta campaign, Cheatham served capably under William J. Hardee. He then took command of Hardee's corps following Atlanta and led it back into Tennessee. This service under Hood, however, gave rise to great controversy, but Cheatham continued to fight with his Tennesseans until the last battle of the Army of Tennessee at Bentonville.

After the war he returned to farming, ran unsuccessfully for the Senate in 1872, became superintendent of Tennessee prisons, and finally postmaster of Nashville, where he died on November 4, 1886.

BURIAL SITE: Section 1, Mount Olivet Cemetery, Nashville. Take Lebanon Pike (U.S. 70) east beyond Fessler's Lane. Cemetery is easily identifiable on right (south).

★ JOSEPH ALEXANDER COOPER ★
Major General, USA

Son of a veteran of the War of 1812, Cooper was born near Cumberland Falls, Whitley County, Ky., on November 25, 1823. Soon after, his family moved to Tennessee and settled on Cave Creek in Campbell County. After receiving a scant education, Cooper enlisted in the 4th Tennessee Infantry and saw action in Mexico. Upon his return he resumed farming.

A former Whig and an active opponent of secession, he became a delegate to the 1861 Union convention in Knoxville. He actively recruited the men of East Tennessee to fight and, as an example, joined the 1st Tennessee Infantry, USA. He proved himself as a soldier and leader at Wild Cat Mountain and Mill Springs. As a result he was made in March 1862 colonel of the 6th Tennessee Infantry. He and his regiment fought at Murfreesboro, Chickamauga, and Chattanooga. Cooper continued to draw the attention of his superiors, and he was promoted to brigadier in July 1864 during the Atlanta campaign. He commanded a brigade and sometimes a division at Franklin and Nashville and ended the war with John M. Schofield in North Carolina. For his meritorious service he was brevetted in May 1865 major general. In 1868 he lost his bid to become a U.S. Senator, but President Grant soon appointed him collector of internal revenue for the Second District of Tennessee. After holding this position ten years, he moved to Stafford, Kan., and bought a farm. Cooper became highly active and prominent in the Baptist church in his later years. He died in Stafford on May 20, 1910.

BURIAL SITE: By the wall and within fifty feet of the Union monument in extreme northeastern corner of the National Cemetery, Knoxville. Exit Interstate 40 on Highway 441 (Convention Center) and proceed into Knoxville. Turn left at light onto Broadway. Proceed .5 mi. north past Old Gray Cemetery on left. After passing Old Gray, immediately turn left on Pruett and proceed one block to entrance at intersection of Pruett and Tyson.

★ JOEL ALLEN DEWEY ★
Brigadier General, USA

A native of Vermont, Dewey was born September 20, 1840. His family moved to Ohio and he enrolled in Oberlin College. Dewey, the college student, volunteered in the fall of 1861 and became a lieutenant in the 58th Ohio Infantry. In 1862 he transferred to the 43rd Ohio as a captain, remaining with the regiment through its engagements at New Madrid, Iuka, and Corinth. The following spring Dewey became lieutenant colonel of the 111th U.S. Colored Troops, and its colonel in April 1865. He and his regiment spent the last year of the war guarding Gen. William T. Sherman's communications in Tennessee. In November 1865 Dewey was promoted to brigadier general, "the last such appointment made during the Civil War."

Following the war Dewey, though offered a regular commission, left the army and began the study of law in Albany, N.Y. In 1867 he returned to Tennessee, establishing a law practice at Dandridge. Two years later he was appointed attorney general for the Second Judicial district. While at the court house in Knoxville, he had a heart attack and died on June 17, 1873.

BURIAL SITE: Hopewell Presbyterian Church Cemetery in Dandridge. Take exit #417 (Tennessee Highway 92 South) from Interstate 81. Proceed east 2.6 mi. into Dandridge on State Route 92, which becomes Meeting Street. Hopewell Presbyterian Church is located on north side of Meeting St. at intersection with Hopewell St. Cemetery is visible from Meeting St. on high ground behind the church on both sides of Hopewell. Grave is near the road in the section of the cemetery across the street from the church.

⭐ GEORGE GIBBS DIBRELL ⭐
Brigadier General, CSA

*B*orn in White County, Tenn., April 12, 1822, Dibrell received a common school education and spent a year at East Tennessee College in Knoxville. He studied law and was admitted to the bar in 1843. Opening his law practice in Sparta, Dibrell also farmed and ran a store. A member of a strong Unionist family, he became a Union delegate to the state convention in early 1861. When Tennessee seceded, however, he enlisted as a private on the side of the Confederacy and quickly rose to lieutenant colonel of partisan rangers, seeing action at Mill Springs. In 1862 he recruited the 8th Tennessee Cavalry and became its colonel. At Chickamauga he commanded a brigade and remained in command during James Longstreet's Knoxville campaign. Dibrell and his regiment distinguished themselves under Nathan B. Forrest (*q.v.*) in West Tennessee and North Mississippi, and on several occasions he conducted successful independent operations. On July 26, 1864, he was promoted to brigadier general and assigned to Joseph Wheeler's command. He and his brigade saw continuous action in the Atlanta campaign and resisted Sherman's advance toward the Georgia coast and up into the Carolinas. During the closing days of the war, he was entrusted with the Confederate archives and took great care to see that they were preserved.

Following the war Dibrell distinguished himself as a merchant and banker in Sparta. He served as a delegate to the 1870 Tennessee constitutional convention and represented Middle Tennessee as a Democrat in Congress for five terms

(1875-85). He also developed the Bon Air coal mines and became president of the Southwestern Railroad. He died in his hometown on May 9, 1886.

BURIAL SITE: Old City Cemetery, Sparta. Turn south off West Bockman Way on South Church Street. Cemetery is located one block south of West Bockman Way, at intersection of South Church and Wall Streets, behind the city jail.

★ DANIEL SMITH DONELSON ★
Major General, CSA

*N*ephew of Andrew Jackson and a staunch Democrat, Donelson was born in Sumner County, Tenn., on June 23, 1801. He attended West Point, graduating with first honors, but resigned from the army six months after receiving his commission. He became a planter in Sumner County, with a keen interest in politics. As a Democrat he ran unsuccessfully for Congress in 1843 but did serve as a delegate to the Nashville Convention (1850) and was a member of the Tennessee House (1842-43, 1855-59), serving as speaker in the final session. He attended the Democratic National Convention in Baltimore (1860).

Gov. Isham G. Harris appointed Donelson as adjutant general in the spring of 1861. He became a brigadier general in the Confederate army later that summer, and he was assigned to service in western Virginia under Gen. W. W. Loring, and in Charleston, S. C. under Gen. Robert E. Lee. Donelson joined Braxton Bragg as a brigade commander in the summer of 1862, when the Army of Tennessee was reorganized. He led a brigade of Tennesseans in the Kentucky campaign (1862) and at Murfreesboro. In January 1863 the Confederate War Department gave him command of the Department of East Tennessee. He died at Montvale Springs, Tenn., on April 17, 1863, some five days before his promotion to major general.

BURIAL SITE: Presbyterian Church, Hendersonville. Take Interstate 65 north of Nashville, turn south on Two Mile Parkway\Gallatin Road. Proceed to intersection with U.S. 31 East. Turn east and go @ .2 mi. into Hendersonville. Presbyterian Church and graveyard are at intersection of Sanders Farm and Gallatin Roads on north side of 31E.

★ JOHNSON KELLY DUNCAN ★
Brigadier General, CSA

*T*his native of York, Pa., was born on March 19, 1827, and was graduated from West Point in 1849. Duncan followed the familiar path of many professional soldiers of the day, serving on active duty about six years as an artillery officer. He fought against the Seminoles, saw duty in the Pacific northwest, and went to Louisiana in 1855 as an engineer supervising public construction projects in New Orleans. He became in 1861 chief engineer of the Board of Public Works of Louisiana.

When the Civil War began, Duncan was commissioned in 1861 as colonel of artillery and took charge of the defenses of New Orleans. Promoted to brigadier early the following year, he continued to strengthen Forts Jackson and St. Philip. He failed in his efforts against the Union fleet in April, however, exhorting his men: "We are just as capable of repelling the enemy to-day as we were before the bombardment. . . . All will yet be well." Captured, then exchanged, he joined Braxton Bragg as his chief of staff. But fever claimed him quickly and this well-trained soldier died in Knoxville on December 18, 1862.

BURIAL SITE: Confederate Cemetery, Franklin. Follow U.S. Highway 431 (Lewisburg Avenue) one mile east of Franklin to Carnton Lane. Cemetery adjoins McGavock Family plot on the grounds of the Randal McGavock home, Carnton.

★ RICHARD STODDERT EWELL ★
Lieutenant General, CSA

Native of Georgetown, D.C., Ewell was born on February 8, 1817. He attended West Point, after his brother Tom, and graduated in 1840. He served in the southwest and in Oregon and was promoted to·first lieutenant just before the Mexican War. At Cerro Gordo, Tom Ewell, a reluctant soldier, was killed and Richard built a crude coffin from boards and buried him nearby. Lieutenant Ewell and his friend, Phil Kearny, performed with audacity and distinction at Churubusco. This action won him a brevet promotion.

Ewell resigned from the United States Army in May 1861 and was immediately commissioned a lieutenant colonel of cavalry in the Virginia forces; he was appointed brigadier general in the Confederate army on June 17, 1861. He rapidly became Stonewall Jackson's principal lieutenant, fighting at First Manassas, in the Valley campaign (1862), and at the Seven Days. For his distinguished service, Ewell was promoted to major general in January 1862. "Old Bald Head," as he was affectionately known, lost a leg at the battle of Groveton.

Following the death of General Jackson in May 1863, Ewell took command of the Second corps, leading it at Gettysburg and in the spring campaigns of 1864. After Spotsylvania he left the field for health reasons and assumed command of the defenses of Richmond. Near the end of the war, Ewell returned to the field and was captured at Sayler's Creek, April 6, 1865. Although less than successful as a corps commander, Ewell was commended by Robert E. Lee as "an honest, brave soldier, who has always done his duty well."

After the war Ewell moved to his wife's home near Spring Hill, Tenn., where he farmed until his death on January 25, 1872.

BURIAL SITE: Central section, Old City Cemetery, Nashville. Interstates 40/65 to Exit 210C. One block south to intersection of Nolensville Pike (4th Avenue South) and Oak Street.

★ NATHAN BEDFORD FORREST ★
Lieutenant General, CSA

*B*orn July 13, 1821 in Bedford County, Forrest spent his youth and early manhood in North Mississippi, living in modest circumstances and receiving little schooling. He became a successful planter and accumulated wealth as a slave trader.

Closely identified with Gov. Isham Harris in the spring of 1861, Forrest helped equip Tennessee's Provisional Army and raised and armed a regiment of cavalry. He performed with credit at Fort Donelson and managed to salvage his command from that disaster. He became colonel of the 3rd Tennessee Cavalry and won commendation from his superiors at Shiloh. In July 1862, Forrest became a brigadier general and during that summer and fall conducted successful and highly publicized raids into Tennessee.

In 1863, Forrest operated with the Army of Tennessee, until his conflict with Braxton Bragg. He became major general in December 1863, and his operations in West Tennessee and North Mississippi continued with great success, rallying many troops to his banner. The remainder of the war saw him ceaselessly active: the controversial capture of Fort Pillow, the brilliant victory at Brice's Cross Roads, and the bloody stalemate at Tupelo. He rejoined the Army of Tennessee in November 1864, commanding all cavalry, and remained with that army during its ill-fated Tennessee campaign.

Forrest became lieutenant general in February 1865 and spent the spring hunted by greatly superior Federal forces. In April his command was effectively smashed at Selma, Ala. Generally regarded as the most successful non-professional general of the Civil War, Forrest passed into legend, while his tactics have become an object of study and admiration by military experts.

Following the war he was active in public affairs in West Tennessee but met with financial disaster. He died, widely mourned, in Memphis on October 29, 1877.

BURIAL SITE: Originally buried in Elmwood Cemetery, Memphis, Forrest was reinterred in Forrest Park, Memphis, in 1905. Forrest Park is located on the north side of Union Avenue at the University of Tennessee Medical School (Union Avenue and Dunlap Street).

Photo not available

★ ROBERT COLEMAN FOSTER, III ★
Brigadier General, Provisional Army of Tennessee

Born in Nashville in 1818, Foster was the eldest son of Tennessee Sen. Ephraim H. Foster, Andrew Jackson's private secretary, and speaker of the General Assembly. (Foster was a grandson of Tennessee legislator Robert C. Foster and nephew of politically powerful Robert C. Foster, Jr., with whom he is often confused.) Spending his boyhood in Nashville and graduating from the University of Nashville (1836), Foster read law and was admitted to the bar in Nashville, practicing there until the outbreak of the Mexican War. Nashville's fashionable Harrison Guards–with Foster as their commander–played a conspicuous role in the presidential elections of 1840 and 1844 by rallying Whig support across Tennessee. When war came in the spring of 1846, Foster and his Guards volunteered early, becoming Company L, 1st Tennessee Infantry, under William B. Campell (*q.v.*). They served in Zachary Taylor's campaign along the Rio Grande and at Monterrey in 1846, then participated in Winfield Scott's invasion of Mexico the following spring. He distinguished himself in the fight at Medelin Ridge in late March and continued inland with his command, fighting at Cerro Gordo. Foster returned to New Orleans in May 1847, was mustered out with the other members of his regiment, and resumed his law practice in Nashville, becoming a district attorney general in 1850. He continued to be active in Middle Tennessee politics as a Whig.

When war broke out in 1861, Gov. Isham Harris selected Foster as one of five brigadier generals in the Provisional Army of Tennessee. He commanded the middle division of that army and organized the first camp of instruction in Tennessee. When Tennessee forces were turned over to the Confederacy, however, Foster was not offered a commission. Despite entreaties by Harris and many prominent Tennesseans, Foster, a "bitter enemy of Jefferson Davis," was denied a position, even that of commandant of Nashville. In December 1861, Foster had Tennessee's Confederate congressmen withdraw his application for a commission, and he sat out the remainder of the war.

After receiving a pardon from President Andrew Johnson (*q.v.*) in 1865, Foster was elected recorder of Nashville and a few years later became secretary of the "Widows and Orphans Fund Life Insurance Company." Impoverished, he died of consumption in Nashville, on December 28, 1871. The bullet-riddled flag of the "Bloody" 1st Tennessee Regiment was taken from its case in the Capitol library to shroud his coffin.

BURIAL SITE: Section 6, Mount Olivet Cemetery, Nashville. Take Lebanon Pike (U.S. 70) east beyond Fessler's Lane. Cemetery is easily identifiable on right (south). Foster's grave has no stone.

★ WILLIAM MONTGOMERY GARDNER ★
Brigadier General, CSA

Gardner was born in Augusta, Ga., June 8, 1824, and appointed to the United States Military Academy from that state. He graduated in 1846 and became a lieutenant in the 1st U.S. Infantry. During the following year he served as an officer in the 2nd and 7th Infantry, winning brevet promotions in Mexico for gallant and meritorious conduct at Contreras and Churubusco. After the Mexican War he continued in routine post and frontier assignments, until his resignation from the army in January 1861.

Gardner was commissioned lieutenant colonel of the 8th Georgia Infantry and fought with that regiment at First Manassas, during which he suffered a severe leg wound that virtually eliminated the possibility of further service in the field. Promoted to brigadier while recuperating from his wound, he accepted command in October 1863 of the District of Middle Florida. Arriving too late to participate in the battle of Olustee (Ocean Pond), Gardner succeeded only in ending pursuit of the vanquished Federals. In July 1864 he was appointed commissary of prisoners east of the Mississippi and held that position until early 1865, when he took command of the Department of Henrico, with headquarters in Richmond. Gardner's last fight came on April 12, 1865, at Salisbury, N.C., where his command was overwhelmed in a crushing charge led by Gen. George Stoneman.

Gardner returned to Georgia following the war, crippled by his Manassas wound. He lived at Augusta and Rome, but moved to live with a son in Memphis, where he died on June 16, 1901.

BURIAL SITE: Evergreen Section, Elmwood Cemetery, Memphis. Exit Interstate 240 (Exit #29) onto Crump (Lamar) Blvd. Proceed 2 blocks (.2 mi.) west to Dudley. Turn left (south) and continue down Dudley .5 mi. over the elevated bridge entrance to the cemetery.

★ ALVAN CULLEM GILLEM ★
Brigadier General, USA

*B*orn on the Cumberland River in Gainesboro, Jackson County, Tenn., July 29, 1830, Gillem attended school in Middle Tennessee and in 1847 entered West Point. He graduated in 1851 and joined the artillery service, seeing garrison duty as a junior officer in Florida and Texas until 1861.

During the early months of the Civil War, Gillem served as quartermaster under Gen. George H. Thomas and subsequently Don Carlos Buell. In May 1862 he became colonel of the 10th Tennessee Infantry, USA, but remained in Nashville most of that year as provost marshal and adjutant general of Tennessee. In June 1863 he became brigadier general and actively engaged in suppressing Confederate military activity in Middle and East Tennessee. In 1864 he led troops against East Tennessee Confederate forces, an effort marked by the routing of John Hunt Morgan's command that September. He lent assistance to George Stoneman in the raid into Western North Carolina, commanding a division of his cavalry.

Gillem remained with the army after the war, serving as military commander of Arkansas and Mississippi until transferred to frontier duty in Texas. He led the campaign that smashed the band following the notorious Captain Jack, but the effort so weakened Gillem that he was forced to give up active duty. He died soon after in Nashville on December 2, 1875.

BURIAL SITE: Section 6, Mount Olivet Cemetery, Nashville. Take Lebanon Pike (U.S. 70) east beyond Fessler's Lane. Cemetery is easily identifiable on right (south).

★ GEORGE WASHINGTON GORDON ★
Brigadier General, CSA

*B*orn October 5, 1836, in Giles County, Tenn., Gordon's boyhood was spent in Texas and Mississippi. He returned to the Volunteer State and graduated in 1859 from Western Military Institute in Nashville. Trained as an engineer, Gordon worked for a short time as a surveyor before the Civil War commenced.

Initially appointed drillmaster for the 11th Tennessee, Gordon became by July 1861 the regiment's lieutenant colonel. He served in East Tennessee under Felix K. Zollicoffer (*q.v.*) and E. Kirby Smith (*q.v.*), and was captured at Tazewell in the summer of 1862. Exchanged in time to participate in Braxton Bragg's Kentucky campaign, he was promoted to colonel and fought at Murfreesboro, where he was severely wounded. Once recovered, he led his regiment at Chickamauga, Missionary Ridge, and throughout the Atlanta campaign. For his effective service this young man of twenty-seven was promoted to brigadier general following Kennesaw Mountain. He led a brigade at Jonesboro and into the fight at Franklin, where he was wounded and captured again, remaining a prisoner until the end of the war.

Following the war Gordon began the study of law at Cumberland University and opened a practice in Lebanon but soon moved to Memphis. There he owned and managed a large Mississippi plantation, while continuing to practice law. In 1883 Gordon launched a political career, becoming a state railroad commissioner. Two years later he secured an appointment in the Interior Department, serving four years in Arizona and Nevada. He returned to Memphis in 1889 and became superintendent of schools. In 1906 the citizens of West Tennessee elected Gordon to Congress, where he served three terms. Active in commemorating the "Lost Cause," Gordon co-founded the Southern Historical Society in 1869. In 1910 and the following year, he was elected commander-in-chief of the United Confederate Veterans. He died in Memphis on August 9, 1911.

BURIAL SITE: Fowler Section, Elmwood Cemetery, Memphis. Exit Interstate 240 (Exit #29) onto Crump (Lamar) Blvd. Proceed 2 blocks (.2 mi.) west to Dudley. Turn left (south) and continue down Dudley .5 mi. over the elevated bridge entrance to the cemetery.

★ ELKANAH BRACKIN GREER ★
Brigadier General, CSA

A native of Paris, Tenn., Greer was born on October 11, 1825. His youth was spent in Mississippi, where he volunteered for service in the Mexican War in Jefferson Davis' 1st Mississippi Rifles. Following the war he cast his fortunes with the state of Texas, buying land there and becoming commander of the Knights of the Golden Circle.

The Civil War found him as colonel of the 1st Texas Cavalry. He fought at Wilson's Creek and was wounded later at Elkhorn Tavern. Promoted to brigadier general in October 1862, he served the balance of the war as head of the conscription bureau in the Trans-Mississippi Department. In 1864 he was granted the responsibility of leading the reserve forces of the Trans-Mississippi.

Following the war he remained a citizen of Marshall, Tex., but died on a trip east in DeVall's Bluff, Ark., March 25, 1877.

BURIAL SITE: Turley Section, Elmwood Cemetery, Memphis. Exit Interstate 240 (Exit #29) onto Crump (Lamar) Blvd. Proceed 2 blocks (.2 mi.) west to Dudley. Turn left (south) and continue down Dudley .5 mi. over the elevated bridge entrance to the cemetery.

★ ROBERT HOPKINS HATTON ★
Brigadier General, CSA

*B*orn in Youngstown, Ohio, November 2, 1826, the son of a Methodist minister, Hatton moved in 1835 with his family to Nashville. They re-settled in Sumner County in 1837 and five years later went on to Gallatin. Hatton attended schools in Pennsylvania and Tennessee and graduated in 1847 from Cumberland University in Lebanon. He remained at Cumberland teaching and studying law until 1849, when he became principal of Woodland Academy in Sumner County. He was admitted to the bar in 1850 and opened his law practice in Lebanon. From 1855 to 1857 he represented Wilson County in the Tennessee Assembly as a member of the American or Know-Nothing party. He ran unsuccessfully for governor in 1857, but two years later was elected by the American Party to Congress, serving one term. Hatton opposed secession but went with Tennessee after President Lincoln issued his call for troops.

Hatton organized a company in the 7th Tennessee in the spring of 1861 and became colonel of the regiment in May. He and his regiment were sent to western Virginia, where they served in the Cheat Mountain campaign that summer and fall. In 1862 they saw action under Stonewall Jackson in his winter campaign at Bath and Romney. For his fine performance Hatton was promoted to brigadier general. Eight days after his promotion, on May 31, 1862, Hatton was killed at the head of his brigade at Seven Pines.

★ ISAAC ROBERT HAWKINS ★
Brevet Brigadier General, USA

A native of Columbia, Tenn., Hawkins, born on May 16, 1818, moved west with his parents at an early age to Carroll County, Tenn., where he attended common schools and farmed. He read law and was admitted to the bar in 1843, opening a practice in Huntingdon, the Carroll County seat. After serving as a lieutenant in the Mexican War, he resumed his law practice. A Whig and an outspoken Unionist, Hawkins supported the Constitutional Union Party in 1860 and was a delegate to its convention. He served in February 1861 as a Tennessee delegate to the Washington Peace Conference, before assuming the office of circuit court judge.

By the fall of 1862, Hawkins organized "Hawkins' Horse," the nucleus of the 7th Tennessee Cavalry, USA. In its first action, the regiment was smashed by the cavalry of Nathan Bedford Forrest (*q.v.*) at Lexington, Tenn., where most of Hawkins' men were captured. Paroled and back in action by mid-1863, Hawkins and the 7th remained in West Tennesee for a year but were considered by Gen. Stephen A. Hurlbut "a poor command" led by a "very inferior officer." In March 1864, in a fight against the 7th Tennessee Cavalry, CSA, Hawkins surrendered his command. When paroled, the regiment, again under Hawkins, served out the balance of its time in the backwash of the war, chasing isolated bands of Confederates about central Kentucky. During his Civil War career, Hawkins was imprisoned three times and was one of fifty Union officers placed under the fire of their own guns in Charleston Harbor.

After the war Hawkins was commissioned as chancellor of the Sixth District of Tennessee, but he declined to serve. In 1866 citizens of West Tennessee elected him to his first of three terms as a Republican in Congress. He was a delegate to the Republican National Convention in 1868. The following year the Senate confirmed his appointment as brevet brigadier general. One historian of Carroll County credits Hawkins with being "the man, perhaps, above all others, that saved the State of Tennessee from Reconstruction." Hawkins died in Huntingdon, on August 12, 1880.

BURIAL SITE: From the square in Huntingdon, take State Route 22 south 2 mi. Hawkins Family Cemetery is on top of a gentle rise and marked by a Tennessee Historical Marker on right (west) of highway. Remove cable obstruction by hand and proceed by car 200 yds. west down wide grass path to unfenced graveyard containing 15 graves. Isaac Hawkins' grave is in the center.

★ BENJAMIN JEFFERSON HILL ★
Brigadier General, CSA

*B*orn near McMinnville, Warren County, Tenn., June 13, 1825, Hill studied law but entered the mercantile business in McMinnville. He took an interest in Tennessee politics and was elected in 1856 as a Democrat to the state senate.

Hill became colonel of the 35th Tennessee Infantry upon its organization in September 1861. The regiment distinguished itself under Patrick Cleburne at Shiloh, in Braxton Bragg's Kentucky campaign, as well as at Chickamauga and Chattanooga. In late 1863 Hill ran unsuccessfully for the Second Confederate Congress and was appointed provost marshal of the Army of Tennessee. During John B. Hood's Tennessee campaign, he commanded cavalry competently under Nathan B. Forrest (*q.v.*), and was rewarded on November 30, 1864, with promotion to brigadier general.

Following the war Hill became president of the McMinnville and Manchester Railroad and practiced law in McMinnville, where he died on January 5, 1880.

BURIAL SITE: Old City Cemetery, McMinnville. In center of town, two blocks south of Main Street on South High Street.

★ WILLIAM YOUNG CONN HUMES ★
Brigadier General, CSA

*B*orn in Abingdon, Va., on May 1, 1830, Humes attended the Virginia Military Institute, graduating in 1851. He moved to Knoxville; studied law there, and was admitted to the bar, practicing until 1858, when he relocated to Memphis.

At the outbreak of the war, Humes joined the Provisional Army of Tennessee as a lieutenant of artillery. He fought and was captured at Island No. 10. When exchanged he joined Joseph Wheeler as his chief of artillery. He remained with Wheeler and soon commanded a brigade, then a division of cavalry. He fought effectively throughout the Atlanta campaign and in the raid against William T. Sherman's line of communications. With Wheeler he opposed Sherman's advance through Georgia and into the Carolinas. His last fight was at Bentonville. After the surrender Humes returned to Memphis and resumed his law practice. Later he moved to Huntsville, Ala., where he died on September 11, 1882.

BURIAL SITE: Chapel Hill Section, Elmwood Cemetery, Memphis. Exit Interstate 240 (Exit #29) onto Crump (Lamar) Blvd. Proceed 2 blocks (.2 mi.) west to Dudley. Turn left (south) and continue down Dudley .5 mi. over the elevated bridge entrance to the cemetery.

★ ALFRED EUGENE JACKSON ★
Brigadier General, CSA

Born in Davidson County, January 11, 1807, Jackson early in life cast his fortune with East Tennessee. He attended both Washington and Greenville Colleges and bought a farm on Nolichucky River. He also built an extensive trading empire stretching from North Carolina to Memphis. In addition, he operated mills and stores and engaged in some manufacturing.

At the opening of the Civil War, Jackson became brigade quartermaster under Felix Zollicoffer (q.v.) and exhibited great enterprise collecting stores and equipment for the latter's command. After Zollicoffer's death he served under E. Kirby Smith (q.v.) in the Department of East Tennessee. For his efficiency and energy, Jackson won on February 9, 1863, promotion to brigadier general. He took command of a brigade of infantry in East Tennessee, rendering conspicuous service in September at Telford's Depot. It was this action that won him the nickname "Mudwall." During the fall of 1863, Jackson's brigade was attached to Matt Ransom's division in James Longstreet's ill-fated East Tennessee campaign. After assisting in the repulse of Stephen Burbridge's forces at Saltville the following September, Jackson remained inactive for the remainder of the war.

Following the surrender Jackson returned to East Tennessee and with great difficulty reclaimed some of his prewar estate, before his death in Jonesboro, on October 30, 1889.

BURIAL SITE: From the Washington County Court House in Jonesboro, go east
.2 mi. up Main Street to the intersection with Clay Avenue. Take left fork of Main
St. up hill. Cemetery is on hill on left (north) side of road. Grave is in extreme
north section on a down slope.

★ WILLIAM HICKS JACKSON ★
Brigadier General, CSA

*B*orn in Paris, Tenn., October 1, 1835, Jackson was raised in Jackson, Tenn., where he attended schools, including West Tennessee College. Appointed to West Point in 1852, graduating four years later, Jackson became a lieutenant of mounted riflemen and served five years against the Indians in New Mexico and Texas.

Jackson resigned from the army in May 1861 and accepted a commission as captain of artillery in the Confederate army. At Belmont in November 1861, he could not land his battery but joined the staff of Gideon J. Pillow (*q.v.*) and was severely wounded. Upon his recovery he became colonel of the 7th Tennessee Cavalry. For his conspicuous service in the capture of Holly Springs, Miss., he was promoted to brigadier general in December 1862. The following spring he commanded a division of cavalry, playing a prominent role in the victory at Thompson's Station. Upon the death of Earl Van Dorn, Jackson became commander of the cavalry defending Vicksburg, and he continued in that capacity under Polk in Mississippi and North Georgia.

"Red" Jackson's cavalry division fought throughout the Atlanta campaign and joined Hood in his invasion of Tennessee. In February 1865 he took charge of all of the Tennessee cavalry in Forrest's command and ended the war actively opposing James H. Wilson's expedition deep into Alabama.

Following the war Jackson associated himself with his father-in-law, Gen. William G. Harding, at Belle Meade in Nashville. He gained widespread recognition for the horses he bred and raised on this splendid farm, where he died on March 30, 1903.

BURIAL SITE: Section 13, Mount Olivet cemetery, Nashville. Take Lebanon Pike (U.S. 70) east beyond Fessler's Lane. Cemetery is easily identifiable on right (south) side.

★ ANDREW JOHNSON ★
Brigadier General, USA

*B*orn in Raleigh, N. C., December 29, 1808, Johnson experienced hardship as a youngster and received no formal education but was apprenticed as a tailor. Soon after the death of his father, he moved with his family to Tennessee, settling in Greeneville. He won early political support, because he took the cause of workingmen and on account of his deep-seated opposition to men of wealth and privilege. From his political base in Greeneville, he progressed from local officeholder to Tennessee legislator (1835-39), presidential elector (1840), Tennessee senator (1841-43), and Congressman (1843-53). He was elected governor of Tennessee in 1853 and re-elected two years later. In 1857 Johnson was elected to the U.S. Senate, serving until 1862, when he became brigadier general and military governor of Tennessee. His had been a powerful voice in opposition to secession and the establishment of the Confederacy, and his contributions in holding East Tennessee loyal to the Union cannot be overstated.

As military governor Johnson established headquarters in Nashville and attempted to deal fairly with the people of Middle and West Tennessee, in effect using this territory as a laboratory for recon-struction. In 1864 he was asked by Lincoln to serve as his vice-president, in an attempt to remove the sectional appearance of the Republican party. Only a few weeks after taking office, Lincoln was assassinated and Johnson assumed the presidency. As President, Johnson soon found himself overwhelmed with the problems of postwar reconstruction, his moderate policies toward the South violently opposed by radical leaders within the Republican party. The struggle between Congress and the President culminated in 1868 in his impeachment trial, in which he was found not guilty by one vote.

After leaving the White House in 1869, Johnson returned to active public life three years later, when he ran for Congress but was defeated. In 1874, however, he was elected once again to the Senate, serving only one session before his death on July 31, 1875, at his daughter's home near Elizabethton, Carter County.

BURIAL SITE: Andrew Johnson National Cemetery, Greeneville. From Interstate 81, proceed east on U.S. 11E to Greeneville. Cross Main Street to Andrew Johnson Visitor Center. From center, return to Main St. and go south .6 mi. through Greeneville on State Route 93/U.S. 321 (Main St.), until intersection with Monument Ave. Turn left (south) off U.S. 321 onto Monument Ave. Cemetery is at end of Monument Ave. (.1 mi.). Grave located prominently in central and highest section.

★ BUSHROD RUST JOHNSON ★
Major General, CSA

*T*his man of contradictions was born of Quaker parents on October 7, 1817, in Belmont County, Ohio (near present-day Morristown). Despite his pacifist background, he attended West Point and graduated in 1840. As an officer in the 3rd U.S. Infantry he served in the Seminole and Mexican Wars without distinction, save for extended leaves of absence resulting from illness and a terrible indiscretion as a commissary officer, which blighted his career. He resigned from the army in 1847 and began teaching. He was instrumental in having Western Military Institute moved to Nashville, where Johnson renewed an acquaintance with one of the trustees, Gideon Pillow (*q.v.*).

In the spring of 1861, he became a major in the Provisional Army of Tennessee, working closely with Pillow in organizing that army. He became brigadier general in the Confederate army on January 24, 1862. At Fort Donelson he performed well but again clouded his reputation by walking off the field after the Confederate army had surrendered, thus, technically, breaking his parole. At Shiloh he was wounded leading a brigade. He rejoined the Army of Tennessee and served creditably at Perryville and Murfreesboro and led the Confederate breakthrough at Chickamauga. He cast his fortunes with Gen. James Longstreet thereafter, participating in the ill-fated Knoxville campaign and eventually with his Tennessee brigade joining the Army of Northern Virginia.

Although Bushrod Johnson performed well at Drewry's Bluff and won promotion to major general to rank from May 1864, he revealed a characteristic indecisiveness at the battle of the Crater. Robert E. Lee came to doubt his ability and cast him in a supporting role. Failure at Sayler's Creek on April 6, 1865, led to a mortifying removal from command by Lee.

Johnson's postwar life was a series of business failures until 1870, when he returned to teaching and headed the preparatory division of the University of Nashville. Following the school's failure in 1873, Johnson went with his retarded son to live on a small farm in Macoupin County, Ill., where he died on September 12, 1880. Union veterans paid for his monument and supervised his burial in a cemetery at Miles Station, Ill. In 1975, Johnson's body was moved from this "all-but-abandoned" cemetery and laid to rest next to his wife in Nashville.

BURIAL SITE: Old City Cemetery, Nashville (north central section, City at Mulberry). Interstates 40/65 to Exit 210C. One block south to intersection of Nolensville Pike (4th Ave., South) and Oak Street.

★ ROBERT JOHNSON ★
Brevet Brigadier General, USA

*T*he second son of President Andrew Johnson, Robert was born on February 22, 1834, in Greeneville, Tenn. He attended Franklin College near Nashville for a short while, then he read law and practiced with Robert McFarland of Greeneville. By 1857 the younger Johnson seems to have become his father's secretary and was his political confidant. In 1859 Robert was elected to the Tennessee Assembly, representing the counties of Greene, Hancock, Hawkins, and Jefferson.

An outspoken Unionist, Johnson raised a regiment of East Tennessee volunteers, the 4th Tennessee Infantry, USA, and became their colonel. The regiment was organized in Kentucky during November 1861, and it served primarily in the Cumberland Gap area for about a year, when it withdrew with other Federal forces into Western Virginia. In the fall of 1862, the regiment was converted into the 1st Tennessee Cavalry and joined William S. Rosecrans' army in January 1863. Thereafter, it remained an active and effective part of the Cavalry corps of the Army of the Cumberland.

In late February 1863, Johnson, however, left the regiment and spent the remainder of the war in Nashville on recruiting duty and serving his father, Tennessee's military governor. He officially resigned as colonel of the 1st Tennessee Cavalry on May 4, 1864, and became Andrew Johnson's private secretary. Alcohol blighted the remainder of his life. While President, his father tried desperately to save his son, arranging for the State Department to send him on a mission to investigate the "slave coolie trade" on the African coast and China, a scheme where he would be without drink for an extended period while aboard ship, the U.S.S. *Chattanooga*. Robert, however, seems to have backed out. On June 22, 1867, Johnson was commissioned as a brevet brigadier general, to rank from March 13, 1865.

Toward the end of his father's presidency, Robert spent at least six months in an "asylum" in Washington, D.C., before returning to Tennessee with his family. Soon after their return, he died in Greeneville on April 22, 1869.

BURIAL SITE: Andrew Johnson National Cemetery, Greeneville. From Interstate 81, proceed east on U.S. 11E to Greeneville. Cross Main Street to Andrew Johnson Visitor Center. From center, return to Main St. and go south .6 mi. through Greeneville on State Route 93/U.S. 321 (Main St.), until intersection with Monument Ave. Turn left (south) off U.S. 321 on Monument Ave. Cemetery is at end of Monument Ave. (.1 mi.). Grave in center and highest section beside that of President Johnson.

★ JOHN ENCILL MACGOWAN ★
Brevet Brigadier General, USA

*O*f Scotch and German lineage, MacGowan was born September 30, 1831, in "a log house in the then backwoods" of Smith Township, Columbiana County, Ohio. He received a basic education in the local schools and attended Mount Union and Hiram (Western Reserve) colleges but left before graduation. He moved in 1853 with his family to Steuben County, Ind., where he read law and taught school. He was admitted to the Indiana bar in 1854, then relocated in Davenport, Iowa, where he practiced law. He then returned to Ohio, practicing law and serving as district attorney in Wood County.

In April 1861, MacGowan enlisted as a private in Company B, 21st Ohio Infantry. He became a lieutenant in that regiment but retired when his enlistment ran out in August 1861. A year later he re-entered the army as captain in the 111th Ohio. MacGowan saw little action, remaining for a year on garrison duty at Bowling Green, Ky., then moving with his regiment into East Tennessee under Gen. Ambrose Burnside. He also served as provost marshal of the 3rd Division, Twenty-third Corps.

On March 24, 1864, MacGowan was promoted to major and transferred to the newly-organized 1st U.S. Colored Heavy Artillery. He soon became lieutenant colonel and colonel of the regiment. The 1st was a relatively large unit (between 1,100 and 1,700 men), which served the remainder of the war in various locations between Greeneville, Tenn., and Asheville, N.C. MacGowan was made a brevet brigadier general on March 13, 1865, and mustered out with his regiment the following March in Chattanooga.

Liking Chattanooga, MacGowan decided to make it his home. He opened a law practice and attained success, serving as city attorney and helping develop the town's first title company. In 1872 he entered the newspaper business, joining the staff of the *Chattanooga Times* as associate editor. After several years he went to work for the *Chattanooga Dispatch* and then the *Knoxville Tribune*. In 1878, at the request of Adolph Ochs, MacGowan returned to Chattanooga and became editor-in-chief of the *Times*, a position he held until his death, on April 12, 1903. He was a much-beloved and highly regarded member of the Chattanooga community, civic-minded, and an authority on industrial history and a host of other topics.

BURIAL SITE: Chattanooga Memorial Park. From downtown Chattanooga take U.S. 27 north over the Tennessee River. After crossing river, go .9 mi. north and exit at Dayton Blvd. Proceed north .2 mi. to Memorial Drive. Turn east and proceed .3 mi. to Chattanooga Memorial Park. Take gravel road behind office bldg. (at entrance) .2 mi to fork in road, which is beginning of White Oak Cemetery within Chattanooga Memorial Park. Stop at fork and walk 30 yds. NNW up slope. Grave is in section 7, about fifth tier of graves up the slope from first fork in gravel road.

★ GEORGE EARL MANEY ★
Brigadier General, CSA

*B*orn in Franklin, Tenn., August 24, 1826, Maney attended Nashville Seminary and graduated from the University of Nashville in 1845. During the Mexican War Maney became an officer in the 1st Tennessee Infantry and upon his discharge accepted a commission as 1st Lieutenant, 3rd U.S. Dragoons. Following the war Maney was elected to the Tennessee House and served one term. He turned to the study of law and was admitted in 1850 to the bar in Nashville, practicing there until the Civil War.

Maney began his Confederate service as a captain in the 11th Tennessee, but in May 1861 he was elected colonel of the 1st Tennessee and led his regiment in Robert E. Lee's Cheat Mountain campaign. In January 1861 he served under Thomas J. Jackson at Bath and Romney. After appealing successfully to the War Department to return to Tennessee following the Fort Donelson calamity, he commanded a brigade at Shiloh under Benjamin F. Cheatham (*q.v.*). For his effective work at Shiloh, he was commissioned brigadier general two weeks after the battle. He led a brigade competently and courageously at Perryville, Murfreesboro, Chickamauga, and Chattanooga. In the Atlanta campaign he rose to division command, but at Jonesboro on August 31, 1864, Maney failed and appears to have been relieved from duty.

In 1868, Maney became president of the Tennessee and Pacific Railroad, and in 1876 he was a Republican candidate for governor. He withdrew from the race, however, not wishing to oppose a former comrade, James D. Porter, who eventually was elected. In 1881 he began a thirteen-year career in the diplomatic service, holding posts as U.S. minister to Colombia, Bolivia, Paraguay, and Uruguay. Upon his return from South America, Maney was once again elected to the Tennessee legislature, serving one term in the senate. He died in Washington, D.C., on February 9, 1901.

BURIAL SITE: Section 1, Mount Olivet Cemetery, Nashville. Take Lebanon Pike (U.S. 70) east beyond Fessler's Lane. Cemetery is easily identifable on right (south) side.

⭑ JOSEPH BENJAMIN PALMER ⭑
Brigadier General, CSA

*B*orn in Rutherford County, November 1, 1825, and soon orphaned, Palmer was raised by his grandparents. He attended Union University in Murfreesboro, studied law, and was admitted to the bar in 1848. After opening his law practice in Murfreesboro, Palmer was elected in 1849 as a Whig to the Tennessee Assembly, serving two terms. He also was mayor of Murfreesboro (1855-59).

A staunch Unionist, Palmer resisted secession initially, then he decided to raise a company of infantry for the defense of his state. He quickly became colonel of the 18th Tennessee and led it at Fort Donelson, where he was captured. When exchanged in August 1862, he re-organized his regiment and commanded it at Murfreesboro, where he was thrice wounded. He returned to the regiment in time for Chickamauga, where a severe shoulder wound put him out of action for ten months. When recovered, Palmer rejoined the army at Atlanta to command the brigade of John C. Brown (*q.v.*). At Jonesboro he was wounded once more. Palmer was promoted to brigadier on November 15, 1864, and led ably a consolidated Tennessee-Virginia-North Carolina brigade in Hood's Tennessee campaign. Afterwards, he fought with the army in its last battle, at Bentonville, then marched the Tennessee troops home.

Following the war Palmer resumed his law practice but resisted all attempts by friends to involve him in politics. He died in Murfreesboro, November 4, 1890.

BURIAL SITE: Evergreen Cemetery, Murfreesboro. From square in Murfreesboro proceed .4 mi. east on East Main Street to North Highland Avenue. Turn left (north) and pass Middle Tennessee Medical Center on the right (east). Go one block north and turn right (east) on Greenland Drive. Entrance on north (left) side of Greenland Dr.

★ WILLIAM RAINE PECK ★
Brigadier General, CSA

*B*orn in Mossy Creek (present-day Jefferson City), Tenn., on January 31, 1818, Peck emigrated to Louisiana as a young man and established himself as a plantation owner in Madison Parish. When the Civil War erupted, this successful planter enlisted as a private in the 9th Louisiana Infantry, commanded by Richard Taylor. Transported to Virginia, Peck and his regiment arrived too late to participate in the opening engagement at First Manassas, but for the following four years they saw action constantly.

Peck served successively as an enlisted man, a company commander, and a field officer in Jackson's Shenandoah Valley campaign, the Seven Days, and Second Manassas. The 9th Louisiana and Peck fought at Sharpsburg, Fredericksburg, Chancellorsville, and Gettysburg. Afterwards, Peck became colonel of the regiment and led it through the bloody fighting of 1864. For his conspicuous performance as brigade commander at Monocacy in July, he was praised by Gen. John B. Gordon. The War Department, recognizing his abilities, appointed Peck brigadier general on February 18, 1865.

Paroled at Vicksburg in June 1865, Peck returned to his Louisiana plantation, "The Mountain," where he died on January 22, 1871. He had asked that his body be returned to Tennessee and placed beside those of other members of his family, several of whom had distinguished military records in the wars of the United States.

BURIAL SITE: From Interstate 81 north of Knoxville, take exit #417 (Tennessee Highway 92 North). Proceed 6.7 mi. west to Jefferson City. State Route 92N intersects U.S. 11E and makes a 90° turn right. Continue until the intersection with South Russell Avenue. Turn left and go .7 mi. past Carson-Newman College campus to Andrew Johnson Highway. Turn left on Andrew Johnson Highway and proceed .7 mi. to Westview (Old Methodist Cemetery) on right side of highway. The Peck family graves are in the east section on high ground.

★ GIDEON JOHNSON PILLOW ★
Brigadier General, CSA

*B*orn of fighting stock in Williamson County, June 8, 1806, Pillow was educated at the University of Nashville and early attached himself to the able and popular Gov. William Carroll. He soared to public notice: becoming attorney general of the Ninth District at twenty-five, brigadier general of Tennessee militia at twenty-eight. He read law and developed a successful practice, all the while developing a model plantation in Maury County. His friend, James K. Polk, obligated to Pillow politically, appointed him brigadier, then major general in the Mexican War; roles which Pillow fulfilled adequately as a commander but disastrously as a subordinate.

Pillow, more than any single individual, organized and developed the Provisional Army of Tennessee in the early summer of 1861, and saw to the construction of the defenses of the upper Mississippi River. When the Provisional army was turned over the Confederacy in July, however, Jefferson Davis saw fit to appoint Pillow as only a brigadier general, and he would end the war as such to his deep disappointment. He participated in the miserably coordinated southeast Missouri campaign in late summer 1861, and he talked Gen. Leonidas Polk into seizing Columbus, Ky. He commanded the Confederates at Belmont in November, being badly defeated by the Federals under Grant. Quarreling with Polk, he left the army and went home in January 1862, but returned the following month in the role of savior to Fort Donelson. His actions there forever stained his military reputation.

Pillow sat out the war for most of 1862, suspended from command by President Davis. He returned to lead a brigade in John C. Breckinridge's bloody charge on the last day at Murfreesboro, January 2, 1863. He won the friendship of Braxton Bragg, who charged him with rounding up the absentees of the army– an assignment Pillow performed with striking success in the spring of 1863. Always broadly construing his authority, Pillow ran afoul of the Conscript Bureau in Richmond and was removed. At the insistence of Gen. Joseph E. Johnston, he was placed in charge of conscription in the Western Department in the late summer and fall 1863. Once more clashing with Richmond, he again was re-assigned. He spent the spring of 1864 attempting to organize a cavalry command and led two brigades in June against William T. Sherman's communications at Lafayette, where he was repulsed handily. In the winter of 1865, following the death of Gen. John H. Winder, he temporarily became an energetic and creative commissary of prisoners before ending the war, attempting to gather manpower to refill Johnston's depleted ranks.

Pillow practiced law in Memphis following the war, hounded by creditors who bankrupted him. He died of yellow fever at his plantation in Arkansas, on October 8, 1878, and was first buried "in a swamp."

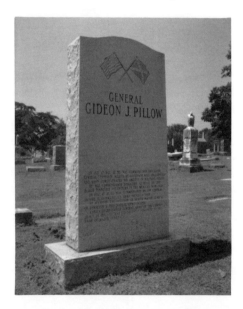

BURIAL SITE: Reinterred probably in the early 1880s at Elmwood Cemetery, Memphis (lot 217, Evergreen). His grave remained unmarked for nearly a century. Exit Interstate 240 (Exit #29) onto Crump (Lamar) Blvd. Proceed 2 blocks (.2 mi.) west to Dudley. Turn left (south) and continue down Dudley .5 mi. over the elevated bridge entrance to the cemetery.

★ LUCIUS EUGENE POLK ★
Brigadier General, CSA

Born at Salisbury, N.C., July 10, 1833, Polk came to Maury County, Tenn., in 1835. He attended the University of Virginia and became a planter in Phillips County, Ark. When war came he enlisted in Patrick Cleburne's 15th Arkansas, serving conspicuously at Shiloh, where he was wounded and won promotion to colonel of the regiment. Wounded a second time at Richmond, Ky., he was promoted in December 1862 to brigadier and the command of Cleburne's brigade. He fought with this distinguished brigade at Murfreesboro, Chickamauga, Missionary Ridge, Ringgold Gap, and in the Atlanta campaign, until Kennesaw Mountain, where he was wounded by a cannon ball so severely that he could not resume active duty.

Polk returned to Maury County and lived there the remainder of his life. In 1884 he was elected delegate to the Democratic National Convention in Chicago and three years later to the Tennessee Senate. He died near Columbia, Tenn., on December 1, 1892.

BURIAL SITE: St. John's Episcopal Church. From court house square at Columbia, go south on U.S. 43 (Columbia-Mt. Pleasant Pike) @ 5 mi. St. John's Church is on left (south), built on the property of Leonidas Polk, Lucius E. Polk's uncle. Cemetery is to left and rear of church. Polk's grave is centrally located along with the graves of the bishops of Tennessee.

★ JAMES EDWARDS RAINS ★
Brigadier General, CSA

*B*orn April 10, 1833, in Nashville, Rains received his basic education locally, before attending Yale Law School, where he graduated in 1854, and opening his practice in Nashville. Soon he became active in the Whig party in Middle Tennessee, being elected city attorney in 1858. Two years later he won election as district attorney for Davidson and two neighboring counties. It was during this period that Rains also served his party as associate editor of the Nashville *Daily Republican Banner*.

In the spring of 1861, Rains enlisted as a private in the Hermitage Guards, Co. D, 11th Tennessee Infantry, and soon rose to captain, before his election as colonel on May 10, 1861. Composed largely of men from Davidson County and West Tennessee, the regiment remained at Cumberland Gap for a year until dislodged from there by the enemy in June 1862. Operating under division commander Gen. Carter Stevenson, Rains, now leading a brigade, distinguished himself not only in the re-capture of Cumberland Gap but also in the October 1862 march to join Bragg's army at Harrodsburg. The 11th did not participate in the fighting at Perryville, but Rains's abilities and services were recognized by his promotion to brigadier general in November. In his first major engagement at Murfreesboro, Rains commanded a consolidated brigade of Tennesseans, Georgians, and North Carolinians under Gen. J. P. McCown. The brigade took part in William J. Hardee's sweeping envelopment on December 31. Leading the extreme left of the Confederate flanking move, Rains eagerly advanced to the front of his brigade but was killed instantly by enemy rifle fire.

BURIAL SITE: Buried on the field at Murfreesboro, Rains's body was reinterred in 1888 in Section 13, Mt. Olivet Cemetery, Nashville. Take Lebanon Pike (U.S. 70) east beyond Fessler's Lane. Cemetery is easily identifiable on right (south). The searcher should not be confused by a metal tablet honoring Rains, which stands near Bushrod Johnson's grave in the Old City Cemetery in Nashville.

★ ROBERT VINKLER RICHARDSON ★
Brigadier General, CSA

*R*ichardson was born November 4, 1820, in Granville County, N.C., and moved first to Wilson County, then Hardeman County, Tenn. He attended Clinton College and taught school for four years, after which he read law and was admitted to the bar. In 1844 he practiced law in Brownsville but the following year came to Memphis. He was colonel of Tennessee militia and during the Mexican War served as an inspector general.

Richardson speculated in land most successfully, owning as much as 100,000 acres in Arkansas. He was a contractor who busied himself constructing levees in Arkansas and Mississippi. When the war came he helped Gideon Pillow (*q.v.*) organize the Provisional Army of Tennessee, and he recruited the 12th Tennessee Cavalry, becoming its colonel. Throughout 1862 he operated under the command of Nathan B. Forrest (*q.v.*) in West Tennessee and saw action at Shiloh and Corinth. The following year he served as brigade commander under James R. Chalmers (*q.v.*) in West Tennessee and North Mississippi. He became a brigadier general on December 3, 1863, though the returns of Forrest's command in 1864 show him as a colonel. In 1864 he remained with Forrest and participated in the Paducah and Fort Pillow raids.

Following the war Richardson moved to New York City and became vice-president of the United States Cotton Company. Spending some time abroad, Richardson returned in 1868 to Memphis, where he became associated with Forrest in railroad building. While inspecting his holdings in southeast Missouri, he stopped for the night on January 5, 1870, at a tavern in Clarkton, Mo. Going out on the porch for a drink of water, Richardson was gunned down by an unknown assassin, who was concealed behind a wagon in the yard.

BURIAL SITE: Chapel Hill Section, Elmwood Cemetery, Memphis. Exit Interstate 240 (Exit #29) onto Crump (Lamar) Blvd. Proceed 2 blocks (.2 mi.) west to Dudley. Turn left (south) and continue down Dudley .5 mi. over the elevated bridge entrance to the cemetery.

★ WILLIAM PRICE SANDERS ★
Brigadier General, USA

*B*orn in central Kentucky on August 12, 1833, Sanders was raised in Natchez, Miss. As the son of a prominent Democrat, he received in 1852 an appointment to the U.S. Military Academy on the recommendation of Gov. Aaron V. Brown of Tennessee. Secretary of War Jefferson Davis interceded on his behalf the following year, when Sanders ran into academic difficulties. After graduation he served in the Second Dragoons until the outbreak of the war, when he was appointed captain of the 3rd U.S. Cavalry and later the 6th Cavalry, seeing action in the Peninsula campaign. Meanwhile, his three brothers fought as members of Confederate cavalry units from Mississippi.

Sanders became colonel of the 5th Kentucky Cavalry, USA, in February 1863, and later in the year chief of cavalry, Department of the Ohio. On October 18, 1863, he was promoted to brigadier general and became actively engaged as a brigade and division commander in Gen. Ambrose Burnside's resistance to James Longstreet's East Tennessee campaign. Sanders was mortally wounded on November 18 in an engagement near Knoxville. He died the following day at the Lamar House in that city.

BURIAL SITE: First buried in the churchyard of Second Presbyterian in Knoxville, Sanders' body was later moved to the National Cemetery, Chattanooga. At intersection of Bailey Avenue and Holtzclaw. Grave is on western slope, Section C, grave #1601.

★ FRANCIS ASBURY SHOUP ★
Brigadier General, CSA

Son of a prominent and well-to-do merchant, Shoup was born March 22, 1835, in Laurel, Ind. He attended Asbury University and then entered West Point, from which he was graduated in 1855. For five years he served as lieutenant of artillery in Florida, then he resigned from the army and began the study of law. In 1861 he settled in Florida and was admitted to the bar.

The war, however, disrupted his plans. Commissioned as a lieutenant of artillery in March 1861, Shoup was summoned by Gen. William J. Hardee to Fort Morgan to help organize volunteers. He went on with Hardee to Arkansas and Kentucky, where he became his chief of artillery. At Shiloh he distinguished himself in that capacity, helping to mass sufficient guns to command the surrender of Benjamin M. Prentiss' command. Following Shiloh he served as a staff officer under P.G.T. Beauregard and then as assistant adjutant general to Thomas C. Hindman at Prairie Grove, Ark. On September 12, 1862, he became brigadier general and took charge of a Louisiana brigade at Vicksburg. Following his capture and exchange, Shoup became chief of artillery for the Army of Tennessee under Joseph E. Johnston. He is credited for not losing a single gun during all the fighting between Dalton and Atlanta. When John B. Hood took charge of the army in July 1864, Shoup became his chief of staff but shortly asked to be relieved.

Following the war Shoup located in Oxford, Miss., where he taught mathematics at the university. In 1868 he became an Episcopal priest and took charge of the parish in Oxford. The following year he went to the University of the South, becoming chaplain and professor of mathematics. He left Sewanee in 1875 to become rector of a church in Waterford, N.Y. He later served parishes in Nashville and New Orleans, before returning to Sewanee in 1883. He remained there as professor of engineering and physics and published one of his four books, *Mechanism and Personality* (1891). He died on September 4, 1896, in Columbia, Tenn.

BURIAL SITE: University Cemetery, Sewanee. From the Sewanee Inn follow University Avenue west .4 mi to Georgia Avenue. Turn left and go .3 mi. Cemetery is on right. Shoup's grave is in section nearest Georgia Ave. Although several sources give Shoup's year of birth as 1834, his carefully carved tombstone insists otherwise.

★ EDMUND KIRBY SMITH ★
General, CSA

*B*orn in St. Augustine, Fla., May 16, 1824, Smith was the son of a New Englander, who distinguished himself in the War of 1812. Smith attended school in Alexandria, Va., before entering West Point, from which he graduated in 1845. He was assigned to the 5th U.S. Infantry and fought with that regiment under Zachary Taylor and Winfield Scott, winning two brevet promotions for gallantry at Cerro Gordo and Contreras. In 1849 Smith became instructor of mathematics at West Point, remaining there until 1852. He then rejoined the 5th Infantry and served with it on the frontier for three years. In 1855 he was chosen as a captain in the select 2nd U.S. Cavalry and fought with this regiment in Indian campaigns in Texas and New Mexico. Wounded in the battle of Nescatunga (1859), he remained with the 2nd Cavalry until 1861 and attained the rank of major.

Smith resigned from the army in March 1861 and was commissioned colonel by the state of Florida. He soon appeared in Virginia, where he became chief of staff to Joseph E. Johnston and assisted in the organization of the Army of the Shenandoah. Promoted to brigadier general in June 1861, he led a brigade at First Manassas, where he was wounded severely. In October 1861 came his appointment as major general and command of the Department of East Tennessee. The following year Smith joined Braxton Bragg in the ill-fated Kentucky campaign, distinguishing himself by winning the battle of Richmond. Despite conflict with Bragg, his performance in Kentucky was rewarded in October 1862 with promotion to lieutenant general.

The following February, Smith took command of the Trans-Mississippi Department and remained in that position until the close of the war. Since he was virtually cut off from Richmond, he truly exercised independent command, the department becoming known as "Kirby-Smithdom." Early in 1864 he became a full general and later that year successfully thwarted Nathaniel Banks's Red River expedition. He surrendered his isolated command in May 1865.

Following the war Smith fled to Mexico then Cuba, before returning in November 1865 to become president of the Atlantic and Pacific Telegraph Company. He soon turned to teaching and for a while operated a school in Kentucky, then became head of the Western Military Academy at Nashville. In 1875 he joined the faculty of the University of the South as professor of mathematics, and he remained in that capacity until his death at Sewanee, on March 28, 1893.

BURIAL SITE: University Cemetery, Sewanee. From the Sewanee Inn follow University Avenue west .4 mi. to Georgia Avenue. Turn left and go .3 mi. Cemetery is on right. Smith's grave is in section nearest Georgia Ave., near the entrance.

★ PRESTON SMITH ★
Brigadier General, CSA

*B*orn in Giles County, Tenn., Christmas Day, 1823, Smith attended local schools, then Jackson College in Columbia. He studied law in Columbia and practiced there until moving to Waynesboro and then to Memphis, where he became a leading member of the bar.

Smith was commissioned colonel of the elite 154th (Senior) Tennessee Regiment and led it effectively at Belmont in November 1861. At Shiloh he was wounded seriously, but returned to duty in time for Braxton Bragg's Kentucky campaign, in which he distinguished himself as a brigade and division commander at Richmond. Promotion to brigadier general came in October 1862. Soon after returning from Kentucky, Smith became ill and missed the battle of Murfreesboro. The following summer at Chickamauga, Smith's position became uncovered by the movement on the evening of September 19 of James Deshler's Texas Brigade. In the darkness Smith rode ahead of his lines, supposing Deshler's Texans to be between him and the enemy. Instead, as he encountered the Union lines, he was recognized as a Confederate officer, and fell mortally wounded, dying on the field. His tombstone indicates that he died on September 20, 1863.

BURIAL SITE: Smith was buried first in Atlanta, then his body was moved years later to Elmwood Cemetery in Memphis, where it is in the Chapel Hill Section. Exit Interstate 240 (Exit #29) onto Crump (Lamar) Blvd. Proceed 2 blocks (.2 mi.) west to Dudley. Turn left (south) and continue down Dudley .5 mi. over the elevated bridge entrance to the cemetery.

★ THOMAS BENTON SMITH ★
Brigadier General, CSA

*B*orn in Mechanicsville, Tenn., February 24, 1838, Smith attended nearby schools, then he entered the Nashville Military Institute, which he attended for four years. When war broke out he was employed by the Nashville and Decatur Railroad. As a junior officer in the 20th Tennessee Infantry, Smith saw action at Mill Springs and Shiloh. Following Shiloh he was promoted to colonel and led his regiment in John C. Breckinridge's ill-fated attack on Baton Rouge. In this battle Smith commanded a brigade and was complimented by Breckinridge for his performance.

At Murfreesboro in December 1862, Smith was again commended, this time by his corps commander, William J. Hardee. Although Smith was disabled at Murfreesboro, he again stood at the head of his regiment at Chickamauga and by May 1864 held brigade command. On July 19, 1864, at the age of twenty-six, he was commissioned brigadier general. He led a Tennessee-Georgia brigade in the remaining battles of the Army of Tennessee and was captured at Nashville. An unarmed prisoner of war in a column of men headed to the rear, he was suddenly attacked and struck across the head by a Union officer brandishing a sabre. From this wound Smith never fully recovered.

He resumed his railroad work and for ten years held jobs as brakeman and conductor. He ran for Congress but failed in 1876. Later that year, probably as a result of his tragic head wound, he was admitted to the state asylum in Nashville, where he drew his last breath on May 21, 1923.

BURIAL SITE: Confederate Circle, Mount Olivet cemetery, Nashville. Take
Lebanon Pike (U.S. 70) east beyond Fessler's Lane. Cemetery is easily identifiable
on right (south) side.

Photo not available

★ WILLIAM JAY SMITH ★
Brevet Brigadier General, USA

*B*orn September 24, 1823 in Birmingham, England, Smith immigrated to the United States as a child and settled in Goshen, N.Y. After attending local schools he served four years in the printer's trade and moved to Tennessee, where he joined James Wheat's Mounted Rangers as they set off to fight in Mexico. Later, as a member of Gen. Winfield Scott's escort, he saw action in all the battles between Vera Cruz and Mexico City. Returning to Memphis he became a painting contractor (1848-58), then purchased a plantation at Grand Junction, Tenn., which he operated until the outbreak of the Civil War.

An outspoken Unionist, Smith was arrested four times by Confederate authorities. He joined the 6th Tennessee Cavalry, USA, becoming quartermaster, and continued to rise through the ranks until April 1864, when he became colonel of the regiment. Somewhat later he took command of a brigade consisting of the 6th and 13th Tennessee Cavalry. Smith participated in numerous actions in West Tennessee and North Mississippi, and he and his regiment were lightly engaged at Nashville (1864). For his services he was brevetted brigadier general in July 1865.

After he was mustered out of the army, Smith became an active public figure. He was a delegate to the Tennessee constitutional convention (1865), a member of the the Tennessee House (1866-67) and Senate (1884-86), and a Republican congressman (1869-71). Afterwards, President Grant appointed him as surveyor of the port of Memphis (1871-83). He invested in real estate, lumber, and banking, before his death in Memphis on November 29, 1913.

BURIAL SITE: Chapel Hill Section, Elmwood Cemetery, Memphis. Exit Interstate 240 (Exit #29) onto Crump (Lamar) Blvd. Proceed 2 blocks (.2 mi.) west to Dudley. Turn left (south) and continue down Dudley .5 mi. over the elevated bridge entrance to the cemetery.

★ JOHN LOUIS TAYLOR SNEED ★
Brigadier General, Provisional Army of Tennessee

*D*escended from a distinguished North Carolina family, Sneed was born in Raleigh, May 12, 1820, and came to Memphis in 1843. He was admitted to the bar and regarded as being unusually well educated. He immersed himself in the life and politics of the Bluff City, becoming in 1846 a member of the board of the University of Memphis and later that year a captain of volunteers in one of the Tennessee regiments. Following the Mexican War, Sneed returned to Memphis, where he served as district attorney general (1851-54) and state attorney general (1854-59).

Sneed, a Whig, was one of the five general officers appointed by Gov. Isham Harris to command the Provisional Army of Tennessee. He was placed in charge of the troops which assembled at Randolph during the summer of 1861. When Tennessee's forces were turned over to the Confederacy, however, Sneed did not receive a Confederate general's commission. Nevertheless, he continued to serve in the army under the command of Albert Sidney Johnston.

Following the war Sneed resumed the practice of law in Memphis, sat on the Tennessee supreme court bench (1870-78), served as an arbitrations judge (1878-83), and established a law school which he operated until his election as chancellor in 1894. He continued in the latter capacity until 1899, when he retired. He died in Memphis, July 29, 1901.

BURIAL SITE: Turley Section, Elmwood Cemetery, Memphis. Exit Interstate 240 (Exit #29) onto Crump (Lamar) Blvd. Proceed 2 blocks (.2 mi.) west to Dudley. Turn left (south) and continue down Dudley .5 mi. over the elevated bridge entrance to the cemetery.

★ JAMES GALLANT SPEARS ★
Brigadier General, USA

A native of Bledsoe County, Tenn., Spears was born on March 29, 1816. Through great industry he managed to receive a basic education and found an opportunity to read law. He opened an office in Pikeville, Tenn., and practiced there. Spears prospered, becoming a landed slave owner. A hard-line Unionist but faithful Democrat, he stood apart from the Confederacy and attended Unionist conventions in East Tennessee, for which he was ordered arrested by Confederate authorities. He escaped to Kentucky in the fall of 1861 and participated in the organization of the 1st Tennessee Infantry, USA, which he led at Wild Cat Mountain and Mill Springs. In March 1861 he was promoted to brigadier and took command of a brigade in the Army of the Ohio. He was active in the campaign for Cumberland Gap and fought as brigade commander at Murfreesboro and at Chickamauga.

Spears opposed vigorously Lincoln's Emancipation Proclamation and his attitude won him arrest and court-martial in early 1864. He was dismissed from the army in the summer of 1864, disdaining an opportunity to resign. Spears sat out the remainder of the war and died a wealthy man, July 22, 1869, at his summer place on Braden's Knob, near Pikeville.

BURIAL SITE: City Cemetery, Pikeville. From the center of Pikeville go south to the junction of Highways 127 and 30. Turn south on 127 and go .2 mi. to Sequatchie Road. Turn west on Sequatchie and proceed .4 mi. to Pikeville City Cemetery. Spears's grave is in the eastern section.

★ TIMOTHY ROBBINS STANLEY ★
Brevet Brigadier General, USA

*S*tanley was born on May 14, 1810, in Hartford, Conn., and was married in 1832 to Prudence Welles. Before 1839 the couple came to Ohio and made their home in Rome township, Lawrence County, where Stanley was the senior partner in a law firm. In 1846, Stanley moved to Jackson, Ohio, where he continued to practice law. The following year he was elected to the Ohio House, representing Scioto and Lawrence counties. From 1848 to 1850 Stanley served as prosecuting attorney in Jackson. Sometime during the 1850s, he relocated to McArthur, Ohio.

Although fifty-one years old, Stanley raised a company in McArthur soon after the war began and helped organize the 18th Ohio Infantry, which elected him as its colonel. The 18th served as railroad guards for three months, before being re-organized in August 1861. The following February, as a part of Buell's Army of the Ohio, Stanley and his regiment followed Gen. A. S. Johnston's Confederate army south through Tennessee into North Alabama. Although it missed Shiloh, the 18th Ohio, in the front line of Negley's division of Thomas' corps, was mauled in the morning fight at Murfreesboro on December 31. The unit rebounded, however, and was conspicuous in the counterattack and pursuit of John C. Breckinridge on January 2. At Chickamauga, the 18th performed well, driving the enemy, but Stanley was struck by shell fragments and disabled. The 18th returned to Chattanooga and remained there for over a year on engineer duty, "building boats, warehouses, mills, and hospitals." Stanley, himself, served as commandant of Chattanooga and lived in the Whiteside home, arguably the finest residence in the area.

Stanley liked Chattanooga, and he brought Prudence down to join him. As a reward for his military service, he was promoted to brevet brigadier general in March 1865. When the war ended, the couple remained in Chattanooga, where Stanley was elected alderman in 1865 and again three years later. He encouraged a group of Ohio friends to provide capital for a bank in Chattanooga. At the time there was neither a bank nor any business of a permanent character. Therefore, the First National Bank, with Stanley as its vice-president, was formed. It quickly was designated as a government depository and in the beginning most of its business was with the U.S. Army. The bank enjoyed success under Stanley's leadership. He was also active in land development, establishing the community of Signal Mountain on Walden's Ridge. Stanley died in Chattanooga on July 8, 1874.

BURIAL SITE: Chattanooga National Cemetery, East of downtown Chattanooga at intersection of Bailey Ave. and Holtzclaw. Grave is on east side of cemetery, at the north end of Section S, with private marker, which faces north.

★ WILLIAM BRICKLY STOKES ★
Brevet Brigadier General, USA

A native of Chatham County, N.C., Stokes was born on September 9, 1814. While his family was enroute to Tennessee in 1818, his father was killed by a runaway wagon. But his mother and her small children continued on to Temperance Hall, Smith (later DeKalb) County, where Stokes eventually became a most successful farmer and livestock breeder. His racehorse, "Ariel," won renown. Stokes entered politics and in 1849 was elected as a Whig to the Tennessee Assembly and was re-elected. From 1855 to 1856 he represented DeKalb and Wilson counties in the Senate. In 1859 he defeated longtime incumbent J. H. Savage for Congress. He made his presence known in Washington, D.C., as a strong Tennessee Unionist with oratorical ability.

When the war came, Stokes waited a year then organized the 5th Tennessee Cavalry, USA, in Middle Tennessee. But as a wag put it, Stokes realized "more success at getting men into the Union army than at getting military discipline into them." Following some success against Confederate cavalry in Middle Tennessee, the 5th fought at Murfreesboro, where it played an important role in repulsing Gen. Joseph Wheeler's attack at Overall's Creek. After Murfreesboro, however, the regiment "never served as a unit," though it rendered important service in detachments throughout Middle and East Tennessee, especially in attacking and dispersing Confederate guerilla units. The regiment's lack of discipline and irregular methods drew the wrath of conventional Federal officers, who demanded that it be sent out of state or disbanded. Finally, in June 1864, the

5th Tennessee was ordered to Tullahoma and Stokes was made commandant of the post at Carthage, where he remained for the balance of the war, carrying mail and chasing guerrillas. President Andrew Johnson (q.v.), who had given Stokes military command in 1862, rewarded him for his faithful service by approving his promotion to brevet brigadier in 1865.

Following the war Stokes returned to Congress in 1866 and served until 1871. While in Washington, the former slave owner introduced the Fifteenth Amendment, which gave freedmen the right to vote. Stokes also studied law and in 1867 was admitted to the bar in Tennessee. In 1871, upon his defeat for re-election to Congress, he became supervisor of internal revenue in Tennessee and greatly expanded his law practice. All the while, Stokes continued to raise racehorses and operate a valuable farm on Smith Fork. He also won recognition as an "excellent fiddler." Stokes died on March 14, 1897, in Alexandria, DeKalb County, his home since 1868.

BURIAL SITE: On Interstate 40 from Nashville to Knoxville, take Exit #254. Head south 7.1 mi. on 141E to State Route 535 to Alexandria. One block off square is High St. At intersection of High and Cemetery Sts., turn east and go .3 mi. up hill to cemetery, which is located behind large blue water tower. At entrance, take right fork. Grave is on left, about 50 yds. from fork.

★ OTHO FRENCH STRAHL ★
Brigadier General, CSA

A native of McConnelsville, Ohio, Strahl was born on June 3, 1831. After graduation from Ohio Wesleyan University, he went south to Tennessee, reading law in Somerville and opening a practice in Dyersburg. When the war began Strahl raised a company of infantry, which was attached to the 4th Tennessee. Early in 1862 Strahl became lieutenant colonel of the 4th and fought with the regiment at Shiloh and Murfreesboro. In January 1863 he became colonel of the regiment and on July 28 brigadier general.

Strahl led a brigade in a division under Benjamin F. Cheatham (*q.v.*) at Chickamauga and performed well. He fought at Chattanooga under A. P. Stewart and returned to serve under Cheatham in the Atlanta campaign and in John B. Hood's invasion of Tennessee. While he was handing muskets up to his sharpshooters at Franklin, he was wounded three times and died on the field.

BURIAL SITE: St. John's Church, Ashwood, Tenn., originally, but in 1901 reinterred in the Old City Cemetery, Dyersburg. From the square in Dyersburg, turn east on Highway 104 (East Court St.). Cemetery is @ .5 mi. east of the square on the south side of East Court St. The grave, conspicuously marked by a large cannon, is in the northwest section.

★ GATES PHILLIPS THRUSTON ★
Brevet Brigadier General, USA

*B*orn on June 11, 1835, in Dayton, Ohio, Thruston developed as a boy an intense interest in collecting and classifying artifacts. He attended Miami University in Oxford, Ohio, graduating in 1855, then he continued his studies at Cincinnati Law School, earning his degree in 1859. At the outbreak of the war, he enlisted in the 1st Ohio Infantry, quickly rising to the rank of captain, and then became ordnance officer on the staff of Gen. Alexander McD. McCook.

Thruston rendered spectacular service at the battle of Mufreesboro, "in the darkest hour" on December 31, 1862. Gen. William S. Rosecrans was astonished, following the collapse of his right wing, to see Captain Thruston approaching the center of the Union line with McCook's ammunition train of 75 wagons in his wake. He had eluded the advancing Confederates and had cut a path through the cedars, reaching the Nashville Pike just in time to avoid capture and to supply the re-formed Union line. Rosecrans, slapping the young man on the shoulder, said to Thruston: "Captain, consider yourself a major from today." A grateful McCook went further, securing additional honors for Thruston, who concluded his military service as judge advocate general for the Army of the Cumberland.

While in Nashville, Thruston fell in love with a girl who had snubbed him and whom he, in return, had labeled a "Secesh scratch-cat." After the war he returned to Nashville and married that girl, and, to please her family, settled there. He was successful in every enterprise he undertook. His law practice flourished, enabling him to retire in 1878 and to spend two years traveling in Europe, "probing ruins." When he returned to Nashville, he accepted the position as president of the State Insurance Company. Thruston involved himself in many business ventures, including founding a cedar bucket company and becoming incorporator of the Nashville, Florence, and Northern Railroad.

His Native American artifact collection continued to grow, and in 1890 he published *Antiquities of Tennessee and the Adjacent States*. His work won him the title of "The Father of Tennessee Archaeology," a bronze medal in Madrid, and a gold medal at the 1904 St. Louis Exposition. He was a benefactor and trustee of many Nashville institutions, earning him the admiration of Tennesseans for his contributions to the study of the aboriginal Indians and his willingness to fight against Reconstruction. His appearances in Washington, D.C., in public opposition to the appointment of a military governor for Tennessee and disenfranchisement of former Confederates only enhanced his popularity. Thruston died in Nashville, his adopted home, on December 9, 1912.

BURIAL SITE: Section 1, lot 162, Mount Olivet Cemetery, Nashville. Take Lebanon Pike (U.S. 70) east beyond Fessler's Lane. Cemetery is easily identifiable on right (south). Grave is 30 yds. from front door of office.

★ ALFRED JEFFERSON VAUGHAN, JR. ★
Brigadier General, CSA

A native of Dinwiddie County, Va., Vaughan was born May 10, 1830. Following his graduation as senior cadet captain from the Virginia Military Institute (1851), he became a surveyor and civil engineer, first establishing himself in St. Joseph, Mo., then moving west and becoming a deputy surveyor of customs in California. For a while, Vaughan served as secretary to a delegation making a treaty with the Indians along the upper Missouri River, before returning east and purchasing a farm in Marshall County, Miss., where he lived until 1861.

When war came Vaughan took a group of neighbors north to Tennessee and became a company commander in the 13th Tennessee Infantry, soon rising in rank to become the regiment's lieutenant colonel. Beginning with the battle of Belmont in November 1861, he fought in all the battles of the Army of Tennessee. For his service at Chickamauga, he was made brigadier general on the field, inheriting the brigade of the fallen Preston Smith (*q.v.*). He saw continuous action during the Atlanta campaign until Vining Station, on July 4, 1864, when a shell exploded near him, severing his left foot and ending his military career.

He returned to farming in North Mississippi until 1872, when he relocated to Memphis. A popular leader of the Grangers, Vaughan served as a criminal court clerk (1878-86). He became active in the United Confederate Veterans, commanding the Tennessee Division. He died in Indianapolis, Ind., on October 1, 1899.

BURIAL SITE: South Grove Section, Elmwood Cemetery, Memphis. Exit Interstate 240 (Exit #29) onto Crump (Lamar) Blvd. Proceed 2 blocks (.2 mi.) west to Dudley. Turn left (south) and continue down Dudley .5 mi. over the elevated bridge entrance to the cemetery.

★ FRANCIS MARION WALKER ★
Brigadier General, CSA

*B*orn in Danville, Ky., on February 1, 1827, Walker read law in Rogersville, Tenn., where he commenced his practice. During the Mexican War he saw duty as a second lieutenant in the 5th Tennessee Volunteers. Walker moved in 1854 from Rogersville to Chattanooga, where he gained prominence as a member of the bar. Gov. Isham G. Harris appointed him in 1858 as state attorney general.

When war broke out Walker organized the Marsh Blues, which became Company I, 19th Tennessee Infantry. Walker became lieutenant colonel of the regiment and participated with it at Mill Springs under Felix Zollicoffer (*q.v.*). That April, in the fight at Shiloh, Walker and the 19th won distinction for accepting the surrender at the "Hornet's Nest" of division commander Gen. Benjamin Prentiss. For his performance Walker was promoted to colonel of the 19th. At Murfreesboro the following December, Walker's regiment fought hard and effectively but lost one-third of its numbers. At Chickamauga the regiment again suffered high casualties. Two months later, at Missionary Ridge, the 19th was overrun while attempting to hold its position.

Gens. William J. Hardee and Joseph E. Johnston appreciated Walker's leadership skills, and in June 1864 he was placed in charge of the brigade formerly commanded by George E. Maney (*q.v.*). In this new capacity, Walker staved off the Federal advance on the "Dead Angle" during the fight for Kennesaw Mountain. He was promoted to brigadier general on July 21 but did not live long enough to see his commission confirmed by the Confederate Senate.

The following day, at the head of the 19th, Walker was killed as Hardee's corps tried unsuccessfuly to turn Sherman's flank at Atlanta.

BURIAL SITE: Walker was buried at Griffin, Ga., with other members of his regiment, but his body was reinterred on October 31, 1889, in Section 3, Forest Hills Cemetery, located at the foot of Lookout Mountain on Tennessee Avenue, just east of U.S. Highway 27.

★ LUCIUS MARSHALL WALKER ★
Brigadier General, CSA

Younger brother of the influential J. Knox Walker and nephew of President James K. Polk, "Marsh" Walker was born on October 18, 1829, in Columbia, Tenn. He attended West Point, graduating in 1850, and served two years with a dragoon regiment on the frontier. Following his resignation in 1852, he became a merchant in Memphis.

Walker entered the Confederate army in the spring of 1861, and by November he had become colonel of the 40th Tennessee and commandant of Memphis. He was promoted to brigadier general on March 11, 1862, and assigned to New Madrid, Mo. He fell ill during the retreat from Island No. 10 and, therefore, missed Shiloh. He fought well at Corinth in May 1862, but he so antagonized Braxton Bragg that he did not see active service again until transferring to the Trans-Mississippi Department, where he commanded a brigade of cavalry and participated in Sterling Price's attack against Helena, Ark. A violent quarrel developed between Walker and Gen. John S. Marmaduke, leading to a duel in which Walker was wounded. He died the next day, September 7, 1863, in Little Rock.

BURIAL SITE: Chapel Hill Section, Elmwood Cemetery, Memphis. Exit Interstate 240 (Exit #29) onto Crump (Lamar) Blvd. Proceed 2 blocks (.2 mi.) west to Dudley. Turn left (south) and continue down Dudley .5 mi. over the elevated bridge entrance to the cemetery.

★ JOHN T. WILDER ★
Brevet Brigadier General, USA

Wilder was born in Hunter's Village, Green County, N.Y., on January 31, 1830. When he was fourteen he moved with his family to Columbus, Ohio, and, as an apprentice, learned well the processes of iron manufacturing, later establishing modest foundries in Greensburg and Lawrenceburg, Ind. When war came he enlisted as a private in a battery for which he had cast the cannon in his foundry, but he soon was appointed lieutenant colonel of the 17th Indiana Infantry, becoming its colonel in March 1862. He fought in western Virginia in 1861, participating in the Cheat Mountain and Greenbrier River campaigns, then came west and saw action at Shiloh and Corinth. Commander of the forces at Munfordville in the path of Braxton Bragg's invading forces, Wilder surrendered the town and spent two months in Confederate prisons.

Following his exchange Wilder became in December 1862 a brigade commander. He and his men, known as the "Lightning" or "Hatchet" Brigade (owing to the hatchets they carried), participated in the pursuit of John Hunt Morgan in 1862, then returned to Middle Tennessee armed with Spencer repeating rifles, which Wilder had purchased with borrowed money. The Lightning Brigade performed with conspicuous efficiency at Hoover's Gap in the spring of 1863. At Chickamauga, Wilder and his men were spectacular, shifting from one troublespot to another as an independent command and were the last unit to leave the field. In October 1863, however, illness forced him to the sidelines, and he resigned his commission. The War Department, however, saw fit to promote him to brevet brigadier in August 1864.

Immediately after the war, Wilder settled in Chattanooga, where he engaged in a variety of enterprises and established the first coke iron furnace in the South. Throughout the southern highlands area, Wilder was generally acknowledged as the leader in the development of natural resources. He traveled to England, studying methods of iron manufacturing which might utilize the impure iron ore of East Tennessee. Wilder also resided for twelve years in Knoxville and Johnson City, and he became involved in operating a railroad. He was an inventor, organizer, and a visionary, founding perhaps a dozen East Tennessee mining and iron producing companies. At one time he and his associates owned over 500,000 acres of iron and coal land in the Appalachian area.

Wilder also interested himself in local politics: he was mayor of Chattanooga, postmaster, and a Republican candidate for Congress. He stood for reconciliation and was instrumental in the development of the Chattanooga-Chickamauga National Military Park, the first in the United States. The last home of the restless Wilder was Monterrey, Tenn. He died on vacation in Jacksonville, Fla., on October 20, 1917.

BURIAL SITE: Forest Hills Cemetery, Chattanooga. Located at the foot of Lookout Mountain on Tennessee Avenue, just east of U.S. Highway 27.

☆ FELIX KIRK ZOLLICOFFER ☆
Brigadier General, CSA

*B*orn of Swiss descent, May 19, 1812, the grandson of a Revolutionary War officer, Zollicoffer was raised in Maury County, Tenn. At age sixteen, having received only a limited education, he apprenticed in the printing office of his cousin, A.O.P. Nicholson. Two years later he edited in Paris, Tenn., the *West Tennessean,* which failed. He next worked as a journeyman printer in Huntsville, Ala., and Knoxville, and, at age twenty-three, he returned to Maury County to become editor of the *Columbia Observer.* After fighting the Seminoles as a lieutenant of volunteers (1838), Zollicoffer returned to the *Observer,* then edited the *Mercury and Southern Agriculturalist* of Huntsville, Ala., and in 1842 the *Nashville Banner,* a Whig paper.

Zollicoffer was a prominent Whig leader, holding a number of offices on the state level, including comptroller and attorney general. He was elected to the Tennessee Senate in 1849 and four years later ran successfully for Congress from the Nashville district, holding his seat until 1859. He campaigned against the election of Abraham Lincoln in 1860, stumping instead in New York for John Bell of Tennessee and the Constitutional Union Party. He served as a member of the National Peace Conference in February 1861.

Gov. Isham G. Harris appointed the influential Zollicoffer a brigadier general in the Provisional Army of Tennessee in April 1861, and he became a brigadier in the Confederate army in June. His initial assignment was the District of East Tennessee, where he did his utmost to work for conciliation in that troubled area.

On January 19, 1862, at Mill Springs, Ky., he was killed while accidentally riding into the ranks of the enemy. A widower for five years, Zollicoffer left behind six orphan daughters.

BURIAL SITE: Old City Cemetery, Nashville. Interstates 40/65 to Exit 210C. One block south to intersection of Nolensville Pike (4th Avenue South) and Oak Street.

Civil War Generals Buried in Tennessee

Adams, Charles W. (1817-1878)	Memphis
Adams, John (1814-1864)	Pulaski
Anderson, James P. (1822-1872)	Memphis
Anderson, Samuel R. (1804-1883)	Nashville
Bate, William B. (1826-1905)	Nashville
Beall, William N. R. (1825-1883)	Nashville
Bradley, Thomas H. (1808-1864)	Memphis
Brown, John C. (1827-1889)	Pulaski
Brownlow, John P. (1842-1878)	Franklin
Campbell, Alexander W. (1828-1893)	Jackson
Campbell, William B. (1807-1867)	Lebanon
Carroll, William H. (1810-1868)	Memphis
Carter, John C. (1837-1864)	Columbia
Caswell, William R. (1809-1862)	Knoxville
Chalmers, James R. (1831-1898)	Memphis
Champion, Thomas E. (1825-1873)	Knoxville
Cheatham, Benjamin F. (1820-1886)	Nashville
Cooper, Joseph A. (1823-1910)	Knoxville
Dewey, Joel Allen (1840-1873)	Dandridge
Dibrell, George G. (1822-1888)	Sparta
Donelson, Daniel S. (1801-1863)	Hendersonville
Duncan, Johnson K. (1827-1863)	Franklin
Ewell, Richard S. (1817-1872)	Nashville
Forrest, Nathan Bedford (1821-1877)	Memphis
Foster, Robert C., III (1817-1871)	Nashville
Gardner, William M. (1824-1901)	Memphis
Gillem, Alvan C. (1830-1875)	Nashville
Gordon, George W. (1836-1911)	Memphis
Greer, Elkanah B. (1825-1877)	Memphis
Hatton, Robert Hopkins (1826-1862)	Lebanon
Hawkins, Isaac R. (1818-1880)	Huntingdon
Hill, Benjamin Jefferson (1825-1880)	McMinnville
Humes, Wm. Young Conn (1830-1882)	Memphis
Jackson, Alfred Eugene (1807-1889)	Jonesboro
Jackson, William Hicks (1835-1903)	Nashville
Johnson, Andrew (1808-1875)	Greeneville
Johnson, Bushrod Rust (1817-1880)	Nashville
Johnson, Robert (1834-1869)	Greeneville
MacGowan, John E. (1831-1903)	Chattanooga
Maney, George Earl (1826-1901)	Nashville
Palmer, Joseph Benjamin (1825-1890)	Murfreesboro
Peck, William Raine (1818-1871)	Jefferson City
Pillow, Gideon J. (1806-1878)	Memphis
Polk, Lucius Eugene (1833-1892)	Columbia
Rains, James Edwards (1833-1862)	Nashville
Richardson, Robert Vinkler (1820-1870)	Memphis
Sanders, William P. (1833-1863)	Chattanooga
Shoup, Francis Asbury (1834-1896)	Sewanee
Smith, Edmund Kirby (1824-1893)	Sewanee
Smith, Preston (1823-1863)	Memphis
Smith, Thomas Benton (1838-1923)	Nashville
Smith, William J. (1823-1913)	Memphis
Sneed, John Louis T. (1820-1901)	Memphis
Spears, James G. (1816-1869)	Pikeville
Stanley, Timothy R. (1810-1874)	Chattanooga
Stokes, William B. (1814-1868)	Alexandria
Strahl, Otho French (1831-1864)	Dyersburg
Thruston, Gates P. (1835-1912)	Nashville
Vaughan, Alfred J., Jr. (1830-1899)	Memphis
Walker, Francis M. (1827-1864)	Chattanooga
Walker, Lucius Marshall (1829-1863)	Memphis
Wilder, John T. (1830-1917)	Chattanooga
Zollicoffer, Felix K. (1812-1862)	Nashville

EAST TENNESSEE HISTORICAL SOCIETY
FOUNDED 1834

FIRST FAMILIES OF TENNESSEE

In honor of Tennessee's Bicentennial in 1996, the East Tennessee Historical Society is sponsoring a new heritage program titled "First Families of Tennessee." The purpose of the project is to identify and recognize all descendants of the first residents of the state of Tennessee. Anyone who is directly descended from a person living in Tennessee when the state was admitted to the Union in 1796, or before, is eligible for membership in this permanent remembrance of his family history and the Tennessee Bicentennial.

To qualify for membership in the First Families of Tennessee, the applicant must directly descend from an ancestor who settled in Tennessee prior to June 1, 1796. The applicant must be able to prove descent from the ancestor (male or female) by an acceptable record or records for each generation, including proof for the applicant. Current Tennessee residence is not required.

Applicants who qualify and are admitted to membership in First Families of Tennessee will receive a handsomely designed certificate issued by the East Tennessee Historical Society featuring the applicant's name and the name of the applicant's ancestor. In addition, members of First Families of Tennessee will receive invitations to members-only events and will have an opportunity to contribute to ETHS activities connected with the Bicentennial celebration in 1996.

The information furnished by applicants as proof of lineage will be placed in the McClung Historical Collection. There, as a resource for other researchers and genealogists, it will serve as a valuable addition to the history of Tennessee and a source of information and pride for future generations.

For more information on this exciting project, or for an application form, please contact the East Tennessee Historical Society, 500 West Church Avenue, Knoxville, TN 37902, or call 615-544-5732.

EAST TENNESSEE HISTORICAL CENTER
Corner of Clinch Avenue and Market Street
Knoxville, Tennessee
Phone 615/544-5732